T0196093

Simply Spirit

Andrew van der Peet

BALBOA
PRESS

A DIVISION OF HAY HOUSE

Balboa Press books may be ordered through booksellers or by contacting:

Balboa Press
A Division of Hay House
1663 Liberty Drive
Bloomington, IN 47403
www.balboapress.com
1 (877) 407-4847

Print information available on the last page.

ISBN: 978-1-9822-1918-5 (sc)
ISBN: 978-1-9822-1919-2 (hc)
ISBN: 978-1-9822-1920-8 (e)

Library of Congress Control Number: 2018915179

Balboa Press rev. date: 01/07/2019

Contents

Foreword

Throughout this book I use the term 'God' to refer to the Divine creator of all life or the highest level of power there is, just because it is such a familiar label used in society, but I understand and respect that there are many other names used depending on a person's own belief systems. I personally believe that no matter what name or label you use to describe the highest, most enlightened being or power (whether it be: the Divine, Source, Universal Intelligence, God, Buddha, or Allah), that it is all one and the same power, simply understood in different ways by different cultures. The views and opinions expressed in this book are based on my own personal understanding of life and I would like to emphasize that I believe everyone understands their own unique portion of the entire truth of all creation that ultimately leads us to oneness with it.

During the early years of my spiritual journey I used to ask the god of my understanding questions during moments of quiet contemplation, and then write down the answers that came to me. I had the idea that maybe one day I would write a book about my views and experiences on spiritualism and include these in it, and so you will find these questions with my answers at the end of the last chapter. It has taken me six years to put my notes and journals together and finish off this book, and now that I have finally aligned my intentions with my higher purpose it feels appropriate to share this now.

Although the grammar, punctuation, organization of content, etc. in this book is far from professional, my desire is to offer, in my own humble wording, my opinions and understandings of things from a spiritual perspective. Words and writings can be interpreted in so many ways but I hope that this book offers something meaningful and helpful, however great or small, to as many people as possible on their spiritual journey.

Special Thanks

I would like to take this opportunity to thank and give my immense gratitude and appreciation to my teachers and friends from the Divine Light Spiritual Foundation; especially Reverend Alva Folkes, Reverend Truly Dubourdieu, Linda Anderson (who is now in spirit), Bonnie Galka, Reverend Allyson Peacock, and Sharon Henry for all their efforts, teachings, and assistance which has helped me grow and achieve *much wisdom* and *tremendous happiness* in life. Their generosity, patience, and openness continue to be an inspiration for me. May many blessings come to them!

Introduction

The reason I decided to write this book is to release and express what has been inside me and also to share some spiritual understandings with anyone who is looking for some answers or direction in order to discover their own truth in their own way. If just one person finds that only one sentence in this entire book helps them in some way, then I feel that the effort has been worth it. I have sincerely enjoyed compiling the scattered notes I have written over the last few years to create this book in order to share not only with my spiritual family, but hopefully many more of you out there who may resonate with some of these words.

My conscious journey with spiritualism began at the age of 35 when I was feeling very dissatisfied, lost and frustrated with my life. I felt that there was so much more to life and that I should be doing something very different but couldn't for the life of me figure out what that was. I was raised Catholic and never really questioned or challenged that belief system, and didn't realize what a narrow perspective I had on life. To me things were mostly black or white, and something either 'was' or it 'was not', leaving little possibility for grey areas. I figured that my religion was a well-meaning one that had good intentions for its followers, and that giving up an hour or so of my time once a week to listen to the priests sermon wasn't asking very much of me. After all, priests seemed to have sacrificed a lot themselves in order to be priests, such as not having a spouse and children and more freedom to pursue personal interests.

Even though I didn't always resonate with every sermon I heard in church I felt that I was at least making a consistent effort to be a better person, along with the others who regularly attended church service. I felt that since I was prone to boredom, selfishness, and judging, it would be in my best interest to go to church once a week to hear motivating reminders of how to live a good life. But eventually that wasn't enough. It was more a case of unconscious discipline, and it wasn't emanating from the right place. My heart had not yet learned to open and speak up.

Eventually I found myself soul-searching in places that I felt were only for people that society regarded as 'strange' or didn't care very much for. I had watched a tv show about mediumship and spiritualism a couple of times and one night as I was watching, the guest on the show happened to be a deep trance (physical channel) medium. I was very intrigued and called in to the show as they were offering messages from Spirit to anyone interested. I was given a brief reading by this medium which turned out to be very accurate (3 years later as predicted). This was my first real brush with mediumship. From there I found my way to an open circle meditation group hosted by a spiritual foundation, and soon after I attended their divine gathering, and continued attending every week from that moment on.

After finally learning to successfully meditate (I won't say exactly how long but I took long enough), I spent the next three years taking spiritual development classes offered by this foundation and, after that, started learning to teach classes and facilitate meditation groups. I continue to teach to this day with much enthusiasm and gratitude and I feel that I live a much more meaningful life than I ever have before!

1.

Consciousness

The universe is like a hologram consisting of many dimensions or levels of consciousness. Depending on how many levels we 'visit' or know about determines how much awareness we hold within ourselves. When we travel through time what we are actually doing is accessing more levels of consciousness, or becoming aware of more that already is. Everything is now, in the moment. All of our past memories are part of our existing level of consciousness and our 'future' is simply another level of consciousness that we have yet to reach. Our physical world is made out to be a linear path with a starting date (birth) and an end date (death), but this is just an illusion. Our physical life (we have many on the earth plane) is actually just a tiny portion of our awareness and there is so much more beyond the physical that we have yet to realize. Our higher consciousness has unlimited potential and will never cease expanding its awareness.

Our true needs will be met at the appropriate moments. We have free will to choose which routes to take along our life's lessons and experiences but our progress and evolving is determined by how selfless we are in our decisions as well as our reasons for choosing and doing certain things. There are some things in our lives that we can change or avoid and some not, but we can positively influence the level of severity of unpleasant experiences just by asking and giving thanks for it in advance. How we handle difficulties has a huge influence on how much or how little suffering we endure. By listening and paying more attention to our inner guidance we can avoid repeating unnecessary patterns and learn our lessons sooner and with less difficulty. When faced with more than one option we can also choose to go with the most challenging one, if it feels right in our heart or gut, and therefore learn and grow more than we would have if we had chosen an easier way. You must be quick to act on that inner voice or gut instinct though or the ego will try to override it by using fear to keep you from moving forward. Ego is very cunning and very defensive so you need to act fast when your soul is offering you guidance. Do what *you* feel is appropriate and learn from your own decisions and experiences. Learning from your mistakes is good for you because that is how you evolve, but in reality there are no real mistakes. Rather, they are opportunities to grow - it's just that they're not so easy to recognize as such. Our growth in life involves experiences anywhere within the range of most positive to most negative. This is what each of us chose for our soul's purpose and so we must face them in order to move forward. We may be able to avoid certain people or situations, or take the easier path when faced with a difficult situation, but all of us will at some point have to learn and experience the lessons life has for us. Avoiding them won't make them go away and whenever we avoid or don't learn a particular lesson, it will keep coming back and each time it will be more challenging than before. Facing your challenges makes you stronger and helps you evolve which is what we are all here for. We will all raise our consciousness to the God source (or highest power) of all creation no matter how long it takes. No one will ever fail in this because we are all from one and the same Divine Source.

Life works in cycles of consciousness with many different levels of awareness and perceptions all trying to mingle harmoniously so that they can merge into a greater understanding and therefore a higher level of consciousness, until a combined and total understanding of all there is can be realized by all. The separateness grows toward oneness in each and every aspect of our understanding. We need to realize that different parts of ourselves (everyone else is part of us) choose to come in and out of our awareness (journey) through life in order for us all to experience and grow closer to one another until we realize that we are, in the highest sense, one giant bundle of pure unconditional love.

Here's an unusual example of unified consciousness from a physical perspective: The connections of us we choose as parents often play the very important role of teaching and mentoring us as best they can, and tend to remain in our physical world for most of our time spent on earth. The grandmother part of us often dotes over us as children and perhaps a favourite uncle takes us to the candy store whenever he happens to visit. A lot of us also decide to experience being a sibling and after that a spouse in order to learn more complex lessons and become more selfless, so that we can in turn learn to share and love. Eventually, many of us become parents leading to much bigger lessons and experiences, and later still comes further extensions of ourselves in the form of grandchildren. Then we get to do the spoiling as well as living vicariously through these grandchildren's innocent young experiences. And so the cycle completes as we leave the physical world to rejoin with spirit, bringing with all that we have experienced from this lifetime. When I was referring to "us" and all our relatives in the example above, I was referring to the various levels of awareness (or understanding) that took the form of a group of physical beings on earth in order to learn and evolve from each other, and eventually become one with the Divine Source of all life. Think of it as a soul group from the spirit world that chose to divide its consciousness or understanding into parts which then manifested here on earth (as people) so that it could experience lessons and growth, and then return to spirit to unite with God/Source.

Consciousness simply means being in a state of awareness. When you are really conscious you are very much in the here and now and are aware that you are not all the thoughts in your head nor are you the physical body that does things, builds things, or changes things. You realize that you, the real you, are the one who 'sees' yourself (body and mind) doing, making, playing, analyzing, and thinking. You are really the one who is witnessing all of this, but these moments of consciousness are rare for most people and even when they do happen they don't last long. Consciousness can be developed through practice but it requires ongoing dedication and trust. People are so used to their physical senses and environment that most of them find it hard to understand and trust in something that is not tangible or logical. Intellect has gotten in the way of gut feelings and heart-centered guidance, which are both about being present or 'in the moment'. Thinking analytically generally involves directing one's attention to the past and/or future. It also opens the door for ego to influence your decision making via thoughts or feelings of self-preservation. If something seems too risky or unknown ego will often reject it. Unconsciousness happens to us all the time and not just while we're asleep or hung over. It's what happens when we are not living in the moment of right now, this instant.

Being conscious has nothing to do with intelligence and anyone, including someone with Down's syndrome, is capable of achieving consciousness. Just being able to remove yourself (your thoughts) from the physical rat race around you and being aware as you do so, raises your consciousness. When all the thinking in your head subsides and you're left with serenity in that moment, you are conscious. An easy method to help you achieve this is by slowing down your breathing and, in turn, your thoughts as much as you comfortably can. When you breathe s l o w e r and watch your thoughts **v e r y s l o w l y** your thinking subsides.

Consciousness is also about letting go; letting go of the past and the future, and therefore letting go of the need to control your life and your surroundings. It is human nature to want to control your environment, and sometimes the people in it, but this is an unconscious path that leads to stagnation and ending up stuck in a comfort zone, even if it's an enjoyable one! To get out of unconscious living, just ask yourself: "how may I serve the bigger picture (others)?" Then, be still and alert enough to receive an answer, which doesn't always come easily; this takes effort and consistency. Ideally, this should be a daily practice throughout your life. This brings to mind one of my favourite quotes, by Pablo Picasso, which is: "The meaning of life is to find your gift; the purpose of life is to give it away."

Becoming more conscious also involves using your strengths and abilities to help others achieve the same. We must help to 're-member' all the lost (dis-membered) souls back to a unified state of consciousness, for ultimately we are all one. This has been talked about and written about throughout the ages but is still mostly ignored on a daily basis. Consciousness involves change and acceptance every single day; learning to see past all the worldly illusions and accepting and appreciating much more of yourself in the form of other people, regardless of where they are at on a level of consciousness.

2.

Inspiring Truth

One day God and Satan were walking along a path when suddenly God stopped to pick something off the ground. He smiled at it glowing radiantly in His hand. Satan asked, "What do you have there?" "This" God replied "is truth." Satan reached for it and said "let me have that, I'll arrange it for you." This is something I read from a book called 'Journey of Awakening' by Ram Dass quite a number of years ago and I want to share it because it relates so much to our present day society. All our lives we are subservient to false gods (truths); especially ones of the physical form. The real God is the god within - the subtle, loving voice that guides us on our path.

Truth is always evolving, expanding, changing. How we live it is what matters. By accepting who you are and what your truth is and reflecting it in front of others without fear, you are simply being truth in one of its many facets. All of us are part of the great truth of life expressed in its various ways. Truth is not about how much data or facts you can learn and remember, and having or knowing more truth than another is not what's important. Showing love and understanding is a far greater truth than measuring and comparing. We are all portions of life's universal truth and the more of it we can accept the closer we are to it. It is simply what you see or experience at any given moment so just accept (but not necessarily agree with) as much of it as possible, for all paths eventually lead to one. By showing everyone our true selves, straight from the heart, we set ourselves free to grow closer in union with spirit and create better truths for all.

While I was out on a bike ride one day I took a break, sat down on a bench and asked spirit "what is truth?" This is the reply I got. *"Truth is whatever you want it to be. It is what you believe about anything. We all start off with our own truth, but as we evolve we learn to accept that there are other truths held by different people. Even though we don't accept many truths of others, by accepting that we are all portions of truth we come to the realization that all of us are making our own ways back to the universal truth from which we came. We must all find our own truth and live it out every moment so that our souls can evolve as intended. Only self knows what its truth is and everyone is responsible for their own self. Find your truth and live it until you discover a new truth for yourself. Then start living that new truth."*

Truth is what sets you free and expands your wisdom because it shows who you really are. When you live each day according to your own truth you align yourself with the path you're meant to follow and you enable your spirit to evolve and grow. When you do this, you help not only yourself but all those you have ever known. Everyone's truth is sacred and we must respect that in others no matter what their level of understanding is, for we don't know what their souls have chosen to experience and learn. Things are not as black and white as most people may think. What was overwhelmingly considered as truth over 100 years ago may now be recognized as being false. Every so often newer discoveries are changing older truths throughout the world.

Truth is not about right and wrong. If you think about it truth, as understood in our society, is basically an opinion or agreement shared by a majority of people. It may also include some form of evidence to support it. No one has the whole truth and nothing but the truth. People tend to base their own truth on what they were taught while growing up and by what they experienced in life, and many will usually reject anything that does not fit in with their reality or belief system. This is quite natural but also very limiting for society as a whole. Everyone's truth is different and truth is therefore never black or white. Truth will always change because there is always more to it.

This physical world in which we live is such a tiny portion of our vastness and immortality, and what we perceive as limitations and impossibilities in the physical sense are not the case in the higher planes of existence. The physical world may have many limitations as to what is true or not but the spirit world does not, and there are no limitations when it comes to God. Truth is merely a word, with a limited definition and understanding for most people, and the way to discover more truth is to allow everyone else their own truth and to always be open to the possibility of replacing yours. Your own truth has most likely changed a few times during the course of your life and will likely change in ever greater amounts in the future, especially since the global consciousness is rising and more people are becoming aware and evolving faster. Although some may fiercely hold onto their old, limited truths, that is okay. Their awareness is still a part of the entire "truth" of all there is and only they can chose a different or higher truth when they feel ready.

Truth, in the highest sense, is not about proving something to be more correct or accurate than another thing. It is not something exclusive based on majority rule or physical evidence, but rather an all-inclusive state of awareness that is tolerant of all levels of understanding and opinion. Here's a basic example: there are two men, and one lives in an area where the climate is like an icy winter all year round and the other lives on a farm in a land with summer-like conditions all year round. The first man, who has never lived in or seen any other place except the land where he lives, believes that trees are scraggly, lifeless, dull and unattractive. The second man, who has never set foot off his farm, says that trees are lush and beautiful and filled with colourful leaves. From personal experience both men are correct but each one only has a portion of the truth. So it is with every other person - each one of us contains a portion of truth based on our own views and experiences. Truth is still truth whether you or I believe it or not.

Speak and you shall be heard - stay silent and you will be lost. You must share your views and beliefs when it feels appropriate; you need to be heard! Truth is also about being authentic in what you say and do and it should permeate all areas of your life. Your truth is always trying to reveal itself to you and encourage you to act it out so that it can manifest, or become a reality, on this physical plane of existence. Every soul has a truth that must be shared with the world no matter how daunting or challenging that may seem to be. When people are not authentic in their living they cause all kinds of problems for themselves and others. It is every person's duty (spiritual purpose) to openly be their true selves so that the global consciousness can move forward. No matter what your level of understanding, your abilities, or your belief system, it is important to express who you are without fear of comparison or judgment from others. Your very essence serves as a gift to all by offering opportunities for those who cross your path to learn and grow from you.

Even if who you are seems inferior, uninteresting, or pointless to another, your paths have crossed for a reason. The truth that you express is important because it has its place in life; it doesn't have to be proven with hard evidence or supported by scientific reasoning to be considered as having any use or value. You *are* truth, plain and simple!

When you do not live an authentic life according to your

own 'highest and best' values, you are withholding others from experiencing your truth; the people in your life do not get to see who you truly are and what you stand for. By following the herd you stunt your personal growth, which in turn affects the whole. Your individuality and personal beliefs needs expression regardless of how it will be perceived by others. Truth is also energy and therefore it is dynamic - it must flow, and eventually evolve into a new truth. When energy is blocked for too long pressure builds, and eventually causes problems. Just like with healing, when your truth comes to the surface to be released or shared it is better to allow it to take its course, for the benefit and learning of all. Feel proud of who you are before others. Be your truth in all its glory until you feel that it no longer reflects who you are. Then find a new truth that feels appropriate to you at that moment.

Now, by your own truth, inspire yourself every day, in whatever ways you can, to feel more, experience more, and love more. We all enjoy inspiration from many external sources but what about the inspiring qualities we hold within ourselves? Do not wait for other people to inspire you. Instead, create your own inspirations and share them with others. You have as much unique inspiration to offer this world as anyone else regardless of people's opinions of you. We are meant to share our own ideas with the world so that all may benefit and grow from the experience. Inspiring others is a wonderful way of helping the global consciousness to move forward and manifest as life intended. When you feel inspired about something and then act on it you gain more strength and confidence to break through fears and follow your life's path. The more inspiration you give to the world the more others will be encouraged to do the same, resulting in more barriers being overcome and greater progress being made by all. Whenever any of you make spiritual progress everyone else benefits from it even though they are not consciously aware of it. The same goes when one does not move forward or make positive changes, for we are all connected. We need to keep changing and experiencing.

We should also allow ourselves to be inspired by God's love and creations to go out and put our thoughts and desires into action so that we may be a continuous reflection and manifestation of that divine love. And since we are all from the same source of divine intelligence, we all have it within ourselves to be a light and inspiration to the world. The power is already in you; there is no need to depend on others to shine and feel inspired.

Each day take a look around you and ask yourself, "does this place make me feel inspired?" or "does this activity I'm now doing truly inspire me?" If it does, keep growing with it and share it as much as possible. If not, start taking steps to redirect yourself elsewhere for there is no passion in doing something that doesn't make your heart sing. Results may not come instantly, but if the path you're taking feels right your heart will find what it desires. Instead of focusing on other people's passions, take some time to look deep within yourself to discover what your passions are and allow them rise to the surface of your everyday consciousness and encourage you act on them. When you feel inspired to do something it makes it seem effortless and that much more enjoyable because of the energy created by it.

I can feel inspired simply by finding a peaceful spot out in nature and watching the birds or squirrels go about their day, or even just sitting in my back yard looking at the trees. These are the times when my mind is most clear and receptive to the things I receive from my higher consciousness, like the insights in this book being shared with you now. Sometimes I might randomly think of something happy which automatically raises my vibration and opens up a channel for all kinds of inspiring stuff to enter my consciousness. It may be as simple as an idea to go for a bike ride, which then might lead me to pass a stranger by and look her way while having a big smile on my face about something that has nothing to do with her. And even that seemingly insignificant event may cause that stranger to smile too and wonder to herself, "I wonder what he's on? I want some of that." This does occasionally happen with me! That stranger might then take that smile back with her to the store she works at where she suggests to her co-workers that they go out together at the end of their shift to figure out something more creative to do on a weekend. Who knows, one of them may be struck with such a bolt of inspiration that she figures out a way to turn her hobby into a career and also have more time to play with her children over the weekend and teach them a lot of extra things she had always wanted to before.

We can also be inspired by many spiritual masters and other saintly, loving people who have walked this earth but inspiration really does come from within if you simply allow it to. We all have this powerful ability which is a part of our nature. Like attracts like so the more you reflect what truly inspires you about this amazing world the more others will feel attracted to show you what truly inspires them. We all have interests or hobbies or even good ideas to improve things, so instead of keeping them to yourself go out and experiment with putting them into action. You never know who or how many will benefit from it. If you can inspire yourself you can inspire anyone without even trying that hard. If you are still quite new to this, start out by simply grinning at strangers in shopping malls and restaurants and you'll be well on your way. Trust me on this. Don't worry if a few of them don't smile back or give you a strange look. Let your intention do all the work and just be your natural self. The energy you emanate will automatically go out and do its thing.

Don't ever assume that you are not inspiring enough to anyone because you may well be a hero or an angel in someone else's eyes. You may have done something kind for someone ten years ago and since forgotten about it, but who knows what that act has meant for that person and how much it has inspired them in their life. I had an angel right under my nose for decades before realizing it and I even had the pleasure of living in her home with her for over 25 years. This angel came into my life disguised as my Mother and is a huge inspiration to me to this day. Her life started out with humble beginnings but she went on to become a much loved music teacher spreading a lot of joy to a lot of people. I now realize the power of her love and teachings towards myself and others and know that we can all do the same. About 6 months before leaving my family home and the continent permanently, I did something really smart by marrying another angel resulting in further prosperity in my life, whether I recognized it at times or not.

We all have angels in our lives just waiting to help us inspire others in turn. Small things lead to big things just like the mustard seed, and we are all that mustard seed. All that's required is some nurturing from you and the possibilities are limitless. Everything in your life is a result of what you have put into it (both consciously and unconsciously) so just imagine how much more amazing you could make it with the power life has given you.

I'd like to share with you the following impressive example of choosing to be an inspiration. It's a story I discovered many years ago and I don't know who wrote it, but it's called "Lovely Rose at 87" and I've summarized it as follows:

On the first day of school a college professor challenged us to get to know someone we didn't already know. As soon as I stood up a gentle hand touched my shoulder. As I turned around I saw a wrinkled, little old lady with a smile that lit up here entire being. She said, "hi handsome, my name is Rose and I'm 87 years old. Can I give you a hug?" I said of course and as she did I asked her why she was in college at such a young age. She replied, "I'm here to meet a rich husband, get married, and have a couple of kids". I asked her again seriously, curious what may have motivated her to take on such a challenge at this stage of her life. "I always dreamed of having a college education and now I'm getting one!" she told me. Over the course of the year Rose became a college icon and she easily made friends wherever she went. She loved to dress up and she revelled in the attention she got from the other students. She was living it up.

At the end of the semester we invited Rose to speak at our football banquet and I'll never forget what she taught us. As she began to deliver her prepared speech she dropped a few of her pages on the floor. Frustrated and a little embarrassed she leaned into the microphone and said, "I'm sorry I'm so jittery. I gave up beer for lent and this whiskey is killing me! I'll never get my speech back in order so I'll just tell you what I know." She then cleared her throat and said, "we don't stop playing because we're old; we grow old because we stop playing. There are only four secrets to staying young, being happy, and achieving success. *You have to laugh and find humour every day. You've got to have a dream. Grow up by always finding opportunity in change. Have no regrets.* There is a huge difference between growing older and growing up. The elderly usually don't have regrets for what they did, but rather for what they did not do." She concluded her speech by singing 'The Rose' and she challenged us to study the lyrics and live them out in our daily lives.

At the year's end Rose finished the college degree that she had begun all those years ago. One week after graduation Rose died peacefully in her sleep. Over two thousand college students attended her funeral in tribute to the wonderful woman who taught by example that it's never too late to be all you can possibly be.

Although we make a living by what we get, we make a life by what we give. God promises a safe landing, not a calm passage. If God brings you to it, He will bring you through it. May this story inspire all of you to show the world who you are by putting your ideas and feelings into action every day so that you can truly feel your inspiration within as well as share it with others.

If you do not create the cause you will not experience the result. If you have created the cause you will definitely experience the result. I encourage you to be yourself no matter who you are with. Express the way you feel without fear or regret and let your individuality shine as best you can for all those who come into your life. We all have opinions and experiences to share with each other and the more of your own truth you give the better for the whole.

3.

Evolution Of Body,
Mind And Soul

A long, long time ago when people roamed the earth on their bare feet they had no worries, no illness, no vengeance, no hatred, and no knowledge except natural wisdom. They lived free and pure, in harmony with nature. People did not have thoughts of not trusting themselves and simply acted out their feelings in accordance with nature. They lived totally in the moment without assumptions or expectations. Then eventually, people learned about structure and order, and separateness which filled their minds with concern, fear, and expectation. This is where they deviated from the path of natural wisdom to the path of knowledge. Facts, figures, efficiency, multi-tasking, expanding memory retention: these are all repetitive tasks leading back to a moment that is no more. A re-enactment or recalling of a past truth; basically, a loop of activity that keeps repeating itself, without any real change or spiritual growth. Feeling safe rather than feeling alive. We as a society allow 'fear' to influence our lives rather than 'love'. Basically every situation is a direct result of either one of these. Fear of having enough for ourselves, rather than lovingly sharing what we have in the moment. The way we experience life, which includes our thoughts, our words, and our actions, is determined by how much fear or love we have.

But we forget that which is most important. I am speaking of the soul, the evolving flow of its existence. It is most difficult for us to listen to and understand what our soul is seeking. The irony is that we are focused on all the things outside of us, trying to own them or control them for our personal gain or enjoyment when we should be focused on what is inside of us waiting to be expressed and shared with all. We tend to listen to our analytical minds when making decisions and taking actions. This is our dilemma, not understanding that all is one and only by serving all can one be served. We create our own challenges and must evolve from that which we create. Now that more people are becoming aware that they create their own reality, they must accept responsibility for their world around them and create the highest and best expression of themselves each moment going forward. We as people need to move away from separatist, fearful thinking and back to unity consciousness so that we can act and live as one unit (of unconditional love) for that is our highest true essence and our original state of being.

Part of our evolution involves experiencing highs *and* lows in order to fully appreciate and have a greater understanding of things. To do this, it is necessary to experience both extremes or polarities of anything. If we were to only experience the very positive aspects of something there would be no point, and no challenge or effort to that experience, and we would not have the complete understanding or appreciation of it. Negative, or 'bad', experiences as we would call them, have their purpose and are not always mistakes or things which could have been avoided. In fact, they are the opportunities for the highest growth, if we are aware and willing enough to accept and learn from them.

Life is full of choices and risks, and sometimes we need

to take the bigger risk in order to grow more. By that I don't mean doing something purely because it is risky, but rather because we feel that we need to let go of fear and attachment and make room for something new or better for our soul. Things are temporary and we're not meant to stay put and live out our lives in the same familiar routine because it seems to be the safe thing to do. It's ok to feel the fear, but we should not let it stop us from going for something that feels appropriate because that's the only way we will experience and grow. It's what we're meant to do and nowhere are there more opportunities for this than here on earth. This earth is where we learn our toughest lessons but it is also where we have countless opportunities to evolve the most.

We have chosen to live in a world of risks, challenges, uncertainties, disappointments and mysteries and so we must face them and overcome them to the best of our abilities, and once we do we will rejoin the spirit of pure love and compassion from where we all came. In a sense, compassion is a state of being which has no real opposite like emotions do. Emotion basically means 'disturbance' and, as such, is not a true sense of who or what we really are. Emotions are learning experiences which help us grow and evolve through this world as we all make our way back to the understanding and acceptance of oneness with all that is.

We are all having a physical life experience which is usually limited to five or six senses. Many believe that we are physical beings that possess a soul inside our bodies when in fact, we are spiritual beings that are and have always been connected to one another. We are all, in the highest sense, one unified soul of unconditional love that is continually expanding its experience on many different plains of existence. Earth is just one of these plains. There are so many realms and planets where life exists, some physical and others not. Soul evolution has to do with raising its awareness or level of consciousness, and it evolves through the experiences of all the different kinds of life forms in existence.

Many are becoming more and more aware of their soul's presence as people are beginning to realize how they are all affecting each other's lives through their actions, belief systems, fears and judgments. More of us are beginning to re-evaluate what is most important in life and gaining a better sense of where to find true happiness. We receive countless opportunities from the soul each day to live in accordance with God's plan of unconditional love but we find it so difficult to recognize these signs in our busy, competitive, material lifestyle. Yet the soul never imposes its will on us but instead, allows us our free will to do as we wish. If we deviate too far from our spiritual path we may find our lives getting really difficult but we still have the choice of whether to continue as we have been, or reflect on what needs to change in our life and begin making those changes.

The soul retains and learns from every one of its life experiences in various worlds of existence. We are all multi-dimensional beings that possess higher sensory levels of perception than the physical ones we mostly use here on earth, such as telepathy, astro-travel, and mediumship. There are so many ways for the soul to communicate and interact with life through an unlimited variety of experiences.

Consider this: 'evolve' is simply another word for change, and that is exactly what each of us are here to do - it is our soul's purpose to continuously evolve into something else. So instead of letting change scare you or stress you out, learn to go with it and see where it leads you. Use your heart or your gut instinct to help navigate you instead of your mental thoughts. Change is a gift to help us move forward and grow; without it we would stagnate and remain trapped in a circle of routine without learning the lessons that life has in store for us. It may cause feelings of fear and discomfort but that has a lot to do with how we deal with it. The changes that happen in our lives are not the cause of our pain or unhappiness; it is our feelings and reactions to those changes that determine how happy or sad we are and this, in turn, affects our degree of presence.

How many times a day do you find yourself thinking about something that has already happened or is still a future projection or fear? When you do that you are not fully present and therefore not able or willing to change. Change brings us into the unknown or, in other words, the present moment which is exactly where we need to be. Resisting it causes stress and unhappiness but by allowing it to take its course, even if you don't agree with it, you will learn and grow from it and overcome whatever changes in your life. Have you ever taken note of certain things about your life that seem stagnant and unstimulating and yet you just keep repeating them out of habit? Or perhaps you do something not because it stimulates or gratifies your heart but because it offers security and peace of mind? Routine is the real problem, not change, because it stagnates, gives one a false sense of security, and prevents evolving.

Sometimes change just happens to us out of the blue catching us off guard before we can prevent it from happening, and other times it presents itself to us as an option or set of choices. Either way, we can choose to roll with it without trying to rationalize it or we can refuse to accept what is. Going with the flow by doing the best you can in the moment makes it possible for real change and growth to occur but resisting and non-acceptance of what is, prevents you from growing and learning.

Another aspect of change is the proactive creating of it which is also part of our divine nature since we are all co-creators of this world. Now, simply thinking about change or wanting to make certain changes in your life won't make it become a reality for you. You have to seriously choose it and take action each day to enable it to manifest for you. A good way to start is by writing your goals down and placing them where you can easily see them, preferably in an area that you look at first when getting up in the morning. I have mine on my desk, written on a large yellow post-it where I can't miss it. Read them each day and take the steps needed to help make those goals a reality. Keep your goals in mind as often as you can every day and make sure your thoughts and actions are in alignment with them. Act as if those goals are already becoming your reality in the present because what you predominantly think and act does become your reality. The world you are now experiencing is a direct result of your past thoughts and deeds. Also make sure that your goals are aligned with a higher purpose (for the benefit of others and not just yourself).

Don't let the time it takes to make changes deter you because that time will pass by anyway. Change isn't always quick or comfortable but without change there are no more experiences, no more newness, and no more evolving. Just take one moment at a time without fighting what is and do what you can in that moment, but keep doing it consistently and with your full attention. Trust your higher guidance to lead you and don't let past mistakes or perceived failures keep you stuck in routine.

Mistakes are a natural part of life and they can just as easily be called lessons or learning experiences instead. If you take a closer look at that word the first syllable reads "mis" and the second syllable reads "take". So, if you 'miss' a lesson or make what seems like a bad decision you will get another 'take' to make a better choice. If you have chosen something that resulted in your life becoming less desirable (which everyone has done before), you can just as easily choose something different that will make your life more enjoyable. You just have to trust the process of change without needing to understand it all first.

Basically, we can either listen to what I refer to as lower

mind or higher mind. Lower mind involves our thoughts about the physical world and its day to day activities and routines: "what do I have to do today to get what I want?" It's all about self and attempting to control one's life by avoiding risks and choosing what offers more security. This, of course, prevents spiritual growth. Higher mind, on the other hand, is the connection to Source (God). This is how we can tap into our soul and discover what we are meant to do for the good of all. Accessing higher or divine guidance is needed in order to learn selflessness, overcome fear, and fulfill our destiny. It also helps to tame ego and encourage us to interact more cooperatively and harmoniously with others, so that a better world is created for everyone. It's about selflessness and service to a greater good: "How may I serve others? What can I do to create more love, joy, and fulfillment for others?"

In the spiritual (permanent, everlasting) realm, we are all one and the same - all of us are on a path of evolution to oneness (unity consciousness). This physical existence, as experienced in separate human bodies all over the world, is just one of many temporary journeys on the path of learning. From our perspective, we 'see' things as existing 'outside' of ourselves; separated by location or distance, or time (births and deaths for example), yet everything is ultimately one. Physicality, as we perceive it, is temporary - basically we are a combination of ideas, feelings, opinions, desires, and preferences all clumped together and encased in a physical body. Isolated, in some ways, from the understanding and awareness of all that is.

4.

Separateness

This very word speaks of aloneness, dividing, isolating, and cutting off. It involves reducing or excluding something, which is opposite to our highest, truest nature. In this world we have forgotten our connection with all there is and have come to believe that we are all separate and individual beings from one another, and always will be even when we leave our physical bodies and cross over to the other side. This illusion of separateness is what allows us to perceive all the problems our society is facing. As long as we continue to live as individuals with exclusive ideals and fear-based actions we will continue to repeat patterns of selfishness, criticism, disharmony, violence, competitiveness, and fears of not having enough. It is our very actions and thoughts that create our physical reality, so by taking a look at the state of our environment you will get a good idea of what most of its people are thinking and creating. We believe that we should have to compete with each other for the things we want, and gain and hoard as much as we can lest we ever find ourselves without enough someday in the future.

Nothing in existence is separate or inferior. Everything has purpose and everything is a vibration of the whole. Basically, life force energy (or the infinite creative power) is one unified awareness or consciousness. Before we were physically born into this world we still existed - we were simply unmanifested but we were still connected to the whole. In the highest sense, we are all one connected spirit or unified soul group but because of our separate and unique physical bodies and personalities, we have learned to live and function as separate beings and this is part of the illusion of the physical world. All physical matter is temporary and has nothing to do with who you really are. Your true essence is basically a divine spark of Source (the god/highest power of your understanding); in other words, you have the highest infinite source of creation within you.

Some of us believe that our knowledge or viewpoint is higher or better than others and some even try to force their views to be accepted as the only correct way. People tend to confuse wisdom with intellect which can, and often does, lead to feelings of superiority. In judging others as less than equal, a whole bunch of negative traits lie waiting to manifest themselves. If society would just try a different approach to the way they live, speak and think their world would become a totally different reality. By living as though everyone else is part of you (your soul), your actions and concerns would become inclusive of them, your views would expand greatly to allow others their own beliefs, and your newfound tolerance would automatically lead to harmony, kindness and love. And the more unconditionally you love the better your world around you becomes, but it starts with you. You cannot force others to change, but by changing yourself those around you will either change themselves or move out of your life.

Practising a life of unity consciousness allows us to become more compassionate and understanding of a much bigger life picture; but having a sense of separateness to the environment and other people, both near and far, causes us to place value judgments on them based on whether they bring us pleasure or pain or whether those things are agreeable to us or not. And since society in general is conditioned to give their attention mostly to what they don't want, more often than not we end up judging too quickly and disassociating ourselves from those things. But, what I dislike and judge in others is potentially also within me. It is easy mistaking a person's behaviour for who they really are, and thereby 'disowning' them as something separate and inferior to who you are, but all souls come from the same source and we cannot possibly know what their lessons and life purpose entail on this earth. No one is separate from anything else - we are all one pure consciousness expressing in its various forms and degrees.

In the environment I lived in when I was growing up it was very important for me to fit in with the crowd and follow the same behaviours and customs of the people around me. There seemed to be a pretty clear distinction of what was acceptable in society and what wasn't. There were beliefs and behaviours that were agreeable to most of the people in my world and anyone who acted or spoke differently from that was either ridiculed, avoided or gossiped about. Society appeared to display a very group oriented mentality and one with little room for grey area. You either were a good fit with the company of most people you knew or you were considered a bit strange, or sometimes presumed to have personal issues which were the reason for your supposed lack of common sense or understanding. The phrase 'common sense' was mentioned often by people, and it seemed to validate and justify so many things in life. It was as if there was a special manual with all the rules, rights & wrongs, and answers to everything; and anyone who didn't know or follow the teachings of this unseen manual didn't know what they were doing. To me it was as if society expected me to think and act a certain way, and if I happened to feel differently I was encouraged to learn not to. Instead, I was expected to learn how to fit in and do as others did in order to gain acceptance and make progress in life.

Being different felt like a massive handicap for me and the

pressure to conform, especially during my teen years, was a long and difficult struggle. I was quite different from my peers and certainly more sensitive than them. I didn't have the level of aggression or force that they had or their willingness to defy authority and test boundaries. I believed that I had to make myself as likeable as possible in order to be accepted in society. I'm not suggesting that I was more right or better than them; I was simply different from the majority. I also made the assumption that what I was taught was the only truth and that those who had authority over me knew best, and only had my best interests in mind. I saw no reason to question or challenge what I was taught even if it didn't seem quite right to me. My fear of being ridiculed or punished for speaking or acting out my own truth held me back from sharing my true self with the world, which resulted in much stuckness, frustration and isolation.

All I was interested in was harmony and whenever I experienced the opposite I would withdraw, unsure of how to deal with it. I just didn't understand that concept - disharmony made no sense to me. I only realized much later on that this was simply a part of life and that I had to learn how to handle it. Life wasn't punishing me for something I had done wrong, it was simply a challenge or lesson for me to grow from. Although I always had friends I was never as close to any of them as they were to each other. I would only let them get so close, or share my personal thoughts and space up to a point. I still felt like a black sheep and just couldn't understand why I was the way I was, and this caused me to make many judgments about myself which then became my beliefs and therefore my reality. I spent many years experiencing things I had no interest in and living a life that did not reflect who I really was and how I felt. I used most of my energy to survive in a lifestyle that was not suited for me without realizing that there was a better way, if I would only choose it and act on it. I had spent long enough experiencing what I did not want and

I had to change it, because I was living society's truth instead of my own and I was not growing as a person.

Being an individual can sometimes be very challenging, especially when your ideas and beliefs are very different from the majority and are not accepted by those who are near and dear to you. It can be hard to live and openly express your own truth while trying to please or gain acceptance from others. Many of us grew up learning to conform to a certain way of life and accept the truths of our teachers, parents, and friends. I certainly didn't question what I learned or even considered the possibility that there is a different truth for every other person in this world. I used to resent being an individual because it made me feel inferior and excluded in many ways. Not fitting in with the crowd gave me the idea that I was not socially oriented and not as mature as I should be.

In the times past it may have been appropriate for people to live and act more as a collective mentality with each one fulfilling a role based on their gender, age, or position of hierarchy, but at present the opposite seems appropriate. Our world is changing at a faster rate now and more people are becoming more conscious and questioning what their true purpose is. As we become more aware of our higher selves we seem to feel a greater need to express our soul's purpose in an effort to evolve and grow closer to the god of our understanding. We are realizing that we are not here simply to earn a living and survive through retirement. Doing things that you are not passionate about can cost you dearly and it can also adversely affect those around you. Although we are all from one and the same source we are here to express our individual natures in this physical world, whether we are judged positively or not. We must have the courage to speak and live our own truths regardless of anyone's attitude toward us. If we all express our individuality in a loving, selfless way then we will be living as life intended us to.

Separateness is uniqueness, but the originating point and

returning point is the same for everything. Consciousness, or life, is continuously bringing its ideas into manifestation through various forms, all of which are temporary. All that you see around you will eventually cease to be; at least the physical representations of them. This world is merely a physical reflection of separateness in the way we, as humans, perceive. We as a consciousness must work through one earthly illusion after another in order to return to our point of origin, before separateness.

5.

Ego And Its Companions

The ego is connected to our personality but it is not who we really are. It is there for our protection and security in the physical world. It is what we use to defend our beliefs and actions and it also helps us to achieve material goals and get things done, such as designing the latest skyscraper or training diligently for hours each day in order to run a marathon. Ego has a competitive nature and a firm belief that we are all separate from one another, leading it to make you believe that you need to control and dominate things or other people in order to be successful. It is the illusion that all of us are here to overcome. It is our challenge and responsibility to tame it to the very best of our ability, one step at a time, until we understand, love, and act as one; until we truly believe that we are all from the same source. Your daily activities, your job or educational title, your history of experiences and achievements, your family ancestry, and your physical characteristics are not who you really are - these are merely things <u>about</u> you. But ego doesn't understand this, it only knows separateness. Ego is not really 'wrong', it is just unconsciousness. The main aim of ego is survival, at all costs. This isn't personal; ego simply doesn't know any better. Because of this, ego leads you to live and act from a place of fear, selfishness, and judgment.

Ego is our wonderland. Our perspective of how the world appears to be, and how it should be. It places values (good and bad) on things according to personal opinions and preferences. It is all about self-preservation, and putting your own needs first. Unlike your soul's nature, ego always wants to control its environment and its experiences, and ensure a safe passage through all the things you undertake to do. Ego likes security and guarantees; it has expectations of favourable outcomes. The level of ego varies from person to person and can be very subtle in some and so pronounced in others that it totally dominates the way they live and interact with people.

In the grand scheme of life ego is temporary and its influence over us usually ends when our physical bodies die - if we are willing. Your personality or ego doesn't literally die with the physical body; rather it has the opportunity to see past the illusion of existing as a separate self and allow you to awaken to the sense of being of service and at one with everything. This does not necessarily have to happen after physical death, and these days more people are becoming conscious as their egos cease to be as controlling and start to grow more aware.

A close companion and one of the major expressions of ego is greed, and its general definition is described as: *the inordinate desire to possess wealth or objects of value with the intention to keep it for one's self, far beyond the needs of basic survival and comfort. It applies to a markedly high desire for and pursuit of wealth, status and power. It is like a bottomless pit which exhausts a person in an endless effort to satisfy a need without ever reaching satisfaction. Greed is typically used to criticize those who seek excessive material wealth, although it may also apply to the need to feel more excessively moral, social, or otherwise better than someone else. The purpose for greed, and any actions associated with it (such as robbery, trickery, or manipulation), is possibly to deprive others of potential means or future opportunities, or to obstruct them there from. It is a mortal sin in the sense that man condemns things eternal for the sake of temporal things.* This goes against our soul's true nature and it constricts us in so many ways. In my opinion, greed is the biggest disease there is because it has resulted in so much destruction, deprivation, illness, isolation, sadness, and death. It has no boundaries and knows no limits. Being greedy is based on fear (another companion of ego) and concern for oneself above all else, and causes resistance to change, hardened hearts, and separation, among other things. Since fear is such a common experience we need to be extra vigilant about the choices we make and actions we take. Greed can never be satisfied because it is always coming from a feeling of lack and wanting better or more. It is also exclusive and competitive and therefore cuts you off from the whole. When people are greedy they may initially accumulate a lot of material wealth or some form of control over others, but they actually prevent themselves from growing closer to God. Their main reason for being that way is based on a subconscious fear of empowering others; a fear that they have to forfeit something or lose power in order for someone else to gain or progress in life.

Here's an extreme example of the harm that greed and fear has caused. Remember the story about King Herod who ordered all male babies born in Jerusalem to be killed, hoping Jesus would also be killed? He was disturbed when he heard about the birth of Jesus because he feared the loss of his kingdom to the new saviour and that a king greater than him would rule the land. Due to his greed he reacted out of fear that he would lose all his wealth and power. Today's times are different but greed still leaves a destructive path, either emotionally, physically, and/or spiritually.

In order for greed to prosper there always has to be a shortage or loss somewhere, whether it be at the expense of people, animals, or natural resources, and this results in imbalance and disharmony. Greed thrives on separateness and competition, winners and losers, which is completely opposite to our divine nature of unity. By preventing another from receiving or benefiting in any way, you also block yourself from moving forward. On the other hand, when you help others to move forward, you help yourself do the same. When making choices involving others we must always ask ourselves: "am I choosing this out of concern for my own well-being first or out of love and a willingness to assist another?"

6.

⁓

Creating Happiness

Everything that happens in our lives is of our own creation. The physical world is the final stage of all thoughts held by us. If a thought is held with enough energy it must eventually manifest into our reality (the physical world). We are responsible for the things we give our attention to; in other words "you are what you think." Your thoughts are continually manifesting your own reality whether you are aware of this or not. If you are not happy with your life the first positive step is to accept that you are the one responsible for it. You are there for a reason - to learn from experiences. There is no right or wrong, or should have or shouldn't have. These are merely judgments. It's all about your outlook in life no matter where you're at and what you do.

Don't criticize or judge yourself or anyone else for getting you there. Simply decide whether you want to change your reality and, if so, where you want to go. All the steps along the way are actually more important than the end result and it's how we perceive the present moment that enables us to determine our own happiness. If we always focus our attention and happiness on the goal itself then we are not living consciously in the "here and now" and therefore cannot enjoy our creating and happiness in the moment. It is good to have goals but the journey, or steps, along the way should be your primary focus. One doesn't find true happiness from doing or having external things, but rather one chooses to feel happiness within, and then does things. It feels great being served by somebody but doesn't it feel equally as good when you help someone else? One sure way to happiness is to serve others for that is your soul's true nature. Happiness is not something you have to search for or earn. It is innate within you, ready to be expressed in all that you do regardless of how important or mundane the activity. Even doing nothing can bring a sense of happiness. Just being, and appreciating, can put you in this state. One doesn't have to be doing something in order to feel happy.

The more you understand how powerful a being you really are, the more you realize that there really are no limits to your creativity. The only time that life may prevent you from creating a certain reality is if that which you are trying to create is not in the best interest of your spiritual path. A basic example would be: if you were meant to be a priest or guidance counsellor you would find it virtually impossible to become a millionaire. Aside from that, it is also important to understand that you will have to take personal responsibility for all that you do. Whenever you are creating anything, ask yourself who will be benefiting from it and will it be for your highest good. It's all about your INTENTION. The way your life is now is always the result of your true intentions. If your reality seems as though it does not match your intentions you need to take a closer look within to discover what your true intentions are as the universe will always manifest exactly that. If you find yourself not liking the present life you've made for yourself simply start creating something else that reflects who you are in this moment. Remember, we are meant to create continuously as a dynamic force and grow from those experiences. There is no retirement from change or evolution.

If life were to stop evolving and changing it would cease to be life.

Don't hang on to external things which you believe bring you security, happiness or a sense of identity for they are impermanent and should be let go of in order to make room for new things to come into your life. Everything in the physical world is temporary and the old must be destroyed (or let go of) for the new to be created and replace it. It's about the learning experience. Everything that you truly need and know, you have within you - you always have.

We are what we are; nothing more or nothing less than another. We change every minute, every second, into something or someone else because energy is never still; it is constantly evolving as life intended. Everything is energy and therefore a part of life. Nothing in existence is useless or coincidental - it simply is. How we invest our energy is critical to our progress in life. If we are focused or attached to something that is not serving us it impedes our evolution as well as those around us. Make a point of checking what your predominant thoughts are focused on and decide whether they are serving you in a positive way or not. If they aren't, take the first steps to detach yourself from those situations. You may not be able to achieve this right away, but taking that first step is very important towards getting your energy restored so that it can serve you in more positive ways. By focusing on and doing positive things for yourself and others you will gain more positive energy, and as a result will be better able to detach from the things that no longer serve you.

It's not to say that certain situations or people become bad, rather we grow in different directions and need to experience other people and situations in order to evolve. People's energies are continually changing and we have the choice to resist or go with these changes. It may be nice to remain in a comfort zone but these eventually pass and sooner or later we all have to make choices and take actions according to the changes, or opportunities, that life presents us. Yes, <u>all</u> changes are in fact opportunities whether we recognize it or not. Neither good nor bad, just ever changing. This is evolution which can never cease, but only continue to become and express as something else.

Be who you really are and feel the way you truly feel inside no matter what the circumstances. By accepting and dealing with life's challenges you grow stronger and add more value to the world. The more you evolve and the more selfless you become, the more you can help others to do the same. And by keeping this up, life can only get better for all of us. Do whatever makes you happy without fear or distraction from anyone, including yourself. Experience as much as you can without regret and really live life to the fullest. The only regrets we tend to have are the ones where we decided not to act when we had the opportunity. Always do your best no matter what. True happiness comes to us when we don't have any conditions about how we'd like to receive it. When we stop allowing ego to rule our lives and fear to influence our actions and decisions, it makes it much easier to set our needs aside and consider those of others. And very importantly, I find that the majority of things I fear most don't actually happen. Think about that; how many of your biggest fears do actually happen to you?

Whenever I encounter a situation that makes me feel anxious or defensive I try telling myself to surrender to the outcome, whatever it may be, and make the best possible choice that will benefit all concerned. However, it doesn't always work out that way though. It's not my nature to start any kind of conflict but I am human and my ego can be a bit tough to handle with certain personalities (even though it's usually my inner thoughts and not so much my outward actions). But I do realize that I should bless and be thankful for those challenging people for they are there to help me learn and grow just as I am here to help others grow. We all need healing in some way. Just keep practising 'being' happy by putting your best side out there every day and you will find your bliss. Always focus your attention on reaching your highest potential and you'll be sure to find your true joy. Remember that your highest potential is not your job or your social life - it is living and acting on your highest truth, each and every moment. This includes your relationships, work place, home, your health and even what you decide to watch on tv or other social media.

Holistically speaking, we all know why we are here but when we separate ourselves from each other we lose those parts of the whole that guide us on our path. Separation is the illusion which brings fear and disharmony to us all, and once we recognize this fact and change our thoughts and actions to benefit all those concerned we can live happily and in harmony with everything. This is how life really is - it's just that we don't allow ourselves to see it. The truth shall set you free to be happy. By being true to yourselves you are true to all there is, and by doing your best you cannot be judged by yourself or others. You are in charge of how you experience life. If there is something that you are not happy about you have free will to change that. You basically have three choices: you can either accept it completely for what it is, change it if possible, or stop doing it. It's about how you perceive things and how you react.

Life's physical situations keep changing but it is your outlook and attitude that determines your quality of life. We are all each other's teachers, and we are, of course, all equal. How can it be otherwise? If we just live in the moment we can be free and happy. Free of time and free of suffering. It is fear that causes us to relive the past and prevent us from moving forward. Once we understand that true happiness comes from within us and not from the physical things around us, we can go about spreading it around, over and over each day. And the more happiness we give out the more happiness we get back. That is the law of attraction and that is why we need to be aware of what we think, say and do at all times. What we think, we are. What we do to and for others we do to ourselves. Happiness is a choice and it requires effort on our part. It doesn't always come easy but it always comes when you are open to it.

We cannot expect or try to reach a point when our lives will be perfect and we have no more trials and errors, but we can learn to see these experiences for what they are and realize that joy and happiness is a conscious choice. Take it as it comes, good or bad, and you will see the way. Perhaps not right away, but you will eventually. Spirit does not work within our time frame and we must have patience and trust. It's up to spirit to give us what we need and when we need it, even if we don't agree with it. We have no choice but to move forward in life and face our challenges and lessons. But the good news is we can never fail. We all have divinity within us and our spirit is nothing less than perfect, so it would be a good idea to remind ourselves of this each day as we try to remember who we really are while dealing with life's challenges.

Gratitude is a powerful tool that we can all use to experience more joy, happiness and contentment in our lives. It also brings us more inner peace and enables us to focus our thoughts on the things we do want, which of course, is an essential part of achieving our goals. By being grateful we open ourselves up to receive more of the positive things that we already have - things which enrich our lives and make us feel blessed. I'm not specifically referring to material things although there is nothing wrong with those at all. We are all having a physical life experience which includes having and wanting material possessions, but these are merely temporary illusions on the path to evolving closer to God. It is good to have goals as they help us to make an effort to achieve and accomplish, but it is the journey (in other words, the present moment) that we should be most grateful for.

All things are temporary and if we can appreciate them while they are in our possession and still be grateful when they are taken from us, then we will surely be on track with keeping happy and understanding that there is no need to ever feel ungrateful. Without contrast or opposites how could we ever understand gratitude? When things are taken from us or people are removed from our lives we have a natural tendency to get ourselves into a state of chaos. When this happens we don't seem to understand why or what is going on. Yet chaos has order in it. Out of chaos new order and structure emerge, and by recognizing this we are better able to process the changes in our lives and maintain a state of calmness or, even better, just being happy with what we have. We just have to look for the positive in everything and that will help us to deal with whatever comes our way. The more you deal with, learn from and accept, the more you can handle and the greater your capacity to be grateful.

Think about this - if you can focus on positive experiences throughout the day such as the friendships you've made, the most amazing and diverse scenery you've ever seen, the unconditional love you received from someone, or even the things you've done for others that have brought them happiness or peace, you open yourself up to receiving just that because you are what you think. If you choose to do this every day and feel this way every day how grateful would you feel? Well, the more often you do it the more you will feel it, and it only takes a moment to notice that.

I used to compare myself to others all the time in all areas of my life which made it extremely difficult to feel grateful and instead kept me trapped while I focused on all the things I didn't have. This made my life very stressful and prevented me from exploring who I am and recognizing all the blessings in my life. But once I began focusing solely on myself and taking personal responsibility I discovered the way to bring change into my life. Only by showing gratitude for everything

I already had was I able to create opportunities to receive more of what I did want and to feel happy and content with myself. I now realize that having less outside of myself enables me to recognize more inside of myself. Everything you ever need comes from within you and feeling grateful for that will enable you to stay open to receiving more instead of less.

I have a great yet simple exercise for you to try out: get a sheet of paper and write your name down vertically on the left side of the page in LARGE letters so that it takes up the full length of the page. Then, next to each letter of your name write down as many positive words as you can about yourself beginning with that letter. Do this when you're feeling very relaxed, and take your time. Go back to your list a couple more times after you think you're done to make sure you get as many positive words as you can. Once you feel that you have got them all, give your list to your partner, your parents, your best friend or your children, and ask them to write down any positive words about you that you don't already have. Once that's done take a close look at all the words written about you. You'll most likely see a whole bunch of things to be grateful for. And I guarantee that you will feel really good about yourself. You may want to keep your list and stick it on the side of your fridge or somewhere you'll see it every day.

I earn less money than my friends and family members but I have more time to spend on the things I love. I don't shop and buy stuff often or hang out at pubs or restaurants much anymore but I can be great company in just about any setting. I'm more interested in the people I spend time with. My side of the family all live on another continent so I only get to see them every few years, but when I do I feel so fortunate. Although we don't see each other much I still feel blessed just to have them because there are some people who haven't even had parents. And when I do see my parents it usually involves time off work, going on excursions and having fun. I may have a very modest job but I don't have much stress and my health is great too. I don't have it all my way but I have a good balance between work and play.

I strive to do my best at what's required of me while reminding myself how blessed I am for the opportunity. Try to give thanks every day for as many things as you can think of just to give yourself a 'feel good' moment when needed. I'm grateful for the opportunity to earn an income, to have good health, to be able to walk or drive myself to places, to eat good food more than three times a day, to have a home and a garden, and to visit different places and hear the many sounds that life has to offer. I'm also blessed with the family and friends I have, the like-minded people I know, the love I receive from so many and the wisdom life reveals to me in so many ways. I'm grateful for my free will and the unconditional love from Source, and even for the lessons that come my way.

Sometimes less is more. Less busy more peaceful. Less resistance more acceptance. Less chaos more clarity. Less anger more tolerance. Less duties more productivity. Less worry more gratitude. It's about recognition of your gifts to yourself and to others. What is done for one is done for all so it makes sense to be grateful for what you give and not just what you receive. So there's a whole lot more to be thankful for - all the things you say and do to help others each day. I believe that most of us have helped others so many times we couldn't remember them all. Going forward, whenever you find yourself struggling to recognize all the blessings life has given you try focusing on all the positive and helpful things you've done for others. Being in a position to help others is truly a blessing and any contribution you make to improve the life of another is well worth feeling good about.

A definition of 'gratitude' is a feeling or attitude that acknowledges a benefit that one has or will receive. What's interesting to note is that the study of gratitude within psychology only began roughly a couple of decades ago possibly because psychology has usually been focused more on understanding distress rather than understanding positive emotions. People who are more grateful have higher levels of well-being and are generally happier, less stressed, and more satisfied with their lives and social relationships. These people also have higher levels of control over their environment, personal growth and self-acceptance. They also have more positive ways of coping with the difficulties they experience and are more likely to seek support from other people and grow from those experiences. They are also less likely to avoid a problem, deny there is a problem or blame themselves; and they tend to sleep better because they think less negative and more positive thoughts just before going to sleep. They are also more likely to show empathy, generosity and helpfulness, and sacrifice individual gains for the benefit of others.

Appreciating the simple joys you experience can help turn negative feelings into positive ones. If you are having problems at work be glad you have a job. If you're experiencing challenges be grateful your life is not boring. Be glad you don't have everything you desire, for if you did, what would there be to look forward to? Be thankful when you don't know something for it gives you an opportunity to learn. Be thankful for your mistakes for they will teach you valuable lessons. Be grateful for your limitations because they give you opportunities for improvement. Be thankful for each new challenge because it will build your character. Be glad when you're tired because it usually means you've made a difference.

Gratitude is an expression of appreciation for what one has and not for what one wants or needs. It is something which can be deliberately cultivated within and also expressed to others resulting in increased levels of energy and optimism. It does not mean that everything is pleasant and perfect, but if you are willing to change your frame of mind and be completely honest with yourself then you can expect to discover a side of yourself that you were probably unaware of. It is not easy, but nothing great is achieved unless you are willing to put in the effort. The truth is, if you don't think that you are worth the time and effort then who will?

Instead of rejoicing in what we have, we tend to want something more, or better, or different. We can't seem to be happy because we are making comparisons and coveting other possibilities. When this happens our ego is dissatisfied and we feel ungrateful. But when we want something more, or better, or different for the benefit of the community, this may be a manifestation of our devotion or our love and then we are grateful for such commitments. The practice of gratitude enhances satisfaction and counters greed, and it links us to the Divine. It is easy to appreciate the good things but a life of fulfillment comes to those who are also thankful for the setbacks. Gratitude can turn a negative into a positive. Find a way to be thankful for your troubles and discover how they can become your blessings.

7.

Healthy Mind, Body And Spirit

Without a healthy mind one cannot have a healthy soul experience. By that I mean listening to your higher (spiritual) guidance and honouring its expression or manifestation through you, as well as entertaining positive, high vibrational thoughts and doing your best not to focus on fearful or negative thoughts. Consistently practice guiding your thinking and your attitude in a positive light. There are a small number of cases where certain people have virtually no control over their state of mind, but that doesn't mean that their souls are missing out on the experiences that they were meant to have. Your soul needs to express itself and when it is ignored or restricted in any way, blockages are created within your being. And if this goes on long enough these energetic blockages can also manifest physically in the form of various illnesses (or dis-ease). When we are not aligned with what we are meant to be doing our emotions make us aware of this. Our bodies have their own intelligence and they know exactly when and where things are not in harmony or functioning properly. The challenge is to learn to pay attention to what your emotions are trying to reveal to you before they begin to manifest as physical blockages. The sooner we deal with our issues the easier we can improve our mental, spiritual, emotional, and physical well-being and move forward onto higher and greater learning experiences.

Your physical body is a part of your spiritual experience and it is therefore important to take care of it as best you can. You're not expected to be in perfect physical shape with an hourglass figure, but you need to at least respect your body for what it is without criticism, and give it what you feel is most appropriate for its well-being. The quality of the nourishment (attitude, food, rest) you give it will have a direct impact on the quality of its condition and functioning. Everything is a vibration of energy and everything you give to yourself and do to yourself has an effect on you. Let's take food for example: high vibrational (healthy) food is beneficial to your physical well-being, but poor quality, badly processed food will negatively affect you, sooner or later. Even if you are a highly intuitive person who does a lot of energy work, your ability to effectively connect with the higher realms, whether to help yourself or assist others to heal, will be adversely affected if you are not physically well. It makes sense that when you don't feel well you won't feel motivated to do pretty much anything! And even if you force yourself to do something while you feel ill, you will not be as effective or helpful. Treat your body kindly, and don't overwork it or try to force it to perform beyond what it feels capable of or necessary.

Do the same with your mind. Nurture it, stimulate it, and respect its strengths and weaknesses. Have no expectations or judgments of it. Also pay close attention to your thoughts and make sure that you only focus on positive ones, because your thinking is a creative force and what you create, you are. Mind is the builder of your experiences. In other words, whatever thoughts you project from yourself will become your reality and have a direct influence on your well-being. If giving your full attention to your words and actions seems difficult, how much of an effort do you find trying to consciously watch all the thoughts that float through your mind to be? How long can you keep that up for in a day? I've considered trying to time myself on how long I can observe my thoughts before my focus is carried away with them and I become lost in whatever mental movie is going on in my head, but I realize that I probably wouldn't even be aware of when to start or stop the timer. Remaining present-minded enough to focus on what your self is thinking or doing requires a lot of effort on a consistent basis, and I think that most of us tend to reject doing so because the task seems so daunting. But making the effort to focus within and train your mind can be done, just like training your muscles or your tolerance. Anything you are willing to work on can be improved no matter where your starting point is on your journey. We're all heading towards greater enlightenment in our own ways and we are here to support and learn from each other, not focus on each other's flaws and weaknesses.

By directing our focus inward, we give ourselves the opportunity to better recognize what we need to work on or let go of in order to move forward in life, and by doing so the outer world around us will change for the better. As I've said before, thoughts are things that have yet to manifest so if you change the way you think and focus on what your soul is trying to tell you, then that will become your new reality. By choosing to practice self-focus you choose to take charge of your life and be an active and conscious co-creator with the whole, and thereby help improve your own health and well-being. If you do not, then you allow things to simply happen to you and therefore have very little power to bring out all the divine gifts that exist within you that are meant to be shared with the world. Everyone has an abundance of spiritual gifts within them; they have always been there, hidden in the last place you would think to look.

For me, quality is more appropriate than quantity. Limiting the pointless activities in my life and slowing things down improves my self-focus so that I can pay more attention to what I'm doing and why I'm doing it. Haste makes waste. I do the same with my thoughts, taking one moment at a time. If I can't come up with an answer or the solution I need soon, I leave it for a while and move on to the next thing. I don't try to force the timing of things; it's easier to remain open and wait, or try again when my intuition tells me to. We are not always meant to be 'doing'. Sometimes one must just 'be'. I gave up tv a few years ago and haven't missed it at all. I never really needed it - it was just there making background noise or getting me hypnotized into whatever show was on. I would basically zone out on my couch and, an hour or two later, wonder what I had just accomplished. Paying attention to your own thoughts and responses in any given situation helps you to be truly focused in whatever life is giving you to experience in that moment; it allows you to fully absorb the experience or emotion. Look for all the things in your life that you feel take a lot of your attention or effort and re-evaluate their importance or value to you. Decide which ones are merely distractions and not really useful or essential to you and let them go. I'm not only referring to material things: these can also be emotional attachments or resentments, old beliefs that don't work for you anymore, feelings of obligation, dis-approvals of any kind, or even the company of certain people. Look out for anything that can prevent you from bringing out your best and gently turn your focus away from it.

Don't go against your own needs or values. Honour your emotions; let them show you what you need to work on and learn. Allow your feelings to surface in order to be expressed or healed. Your feelings are God speaking to you so you need to pay attention to what those feelings are trying to show you. If you suppress them you will create suffering and your emotions will keep trying to surface sooner or later until you address them. Pain is sometimes inevitable but you can, in most cases, choose how much or how long you continue to suffer. There's no need to suppress or try to force a memory to be forgotten; rather acknowledge it simply as something that once was and leave it behind while you move forward making new memories. What has already happened cannot be changed, but it is behind you. What is yet to happen will always remain unknown. What is happening 'in this moment' is the only thing you need to focus on, and your attitude toward this moment will determine how healthy your experience will be. You do not control life's events but you can control how you respond and deal with them. Do what you love and let your soul guide your actions. Surrender the fruits of your labour.

The Dalai Lama was once asked during an interview what he thought was most strange about mankind. He replied that it is 'man' because he sacrifices his health in order to make money, then sacrifices money in order to recuperate his health, and spends so much time worrying about the future that he does not enjoy the present. This is more true than most people realize!

8.

w

Distractions

This is something that affects our world more and more as society tries to keep up with the latest and most popular trends. Most people tend to 'follow the herd' and try to fit in with the ideals of others in order to feel accepted. Instead of directing their focus inward to discover more about themselves and what they have to share with the world, people get distracted by looking outward for what seems to be appropriate or acceptable to society. The competition and distractions of the physical world capture our attention and prevent us from being and sharing our true divine nature. Instead of getting distracted by the activities or misfortunes of others, focus on what you give your attention to so that you are better able to stay on track with your own path, and the less likely you will find yourself getting pulled into other people's drama. It is way too easy getting distracted by the circumstances of other people's lives and their behaviours.

The media is also a huge distraction that can preoccupy our minds for hours each day. How much tv do you think you watch in a day? Is it mostly showing positive, helpful material or is it usually about accidents, drama, violence and judgments about other people? That's a lot of mind programming going on no matter how entertaining it may be. When something has your full attention your focus is acutely drawn towards it and that is what you will attract more of to yourself. Be mindful of that as much as possible. Practice being more aware and give your attention to the things that will benefit your heart and soul. If you desire more peace and positivity focus on anything to do with those, and make a habit of steering your attention away from anything that is opposite to what you desire. Always be aware of the thoughts you are holding and practice weeding out the ones that don't serve you.

Our personal opinions, ideals, and value judgments we make also add to this dilemma. Because of our intolerance or fear of new or foreign concepts and belief systems, we tend to believe that we are all separate from one another, competing for acceptance from the higher powers that be. Deep emotional issues which we are unable or unsure of how to overcome by ourselves are also a major factor that distracts us from focusing on who we are at the soul level and what we should be doing in the present. Instead of accepting and working through emotions as they occur, people tend to bury them and ignore them when they surface in order to be resolved or healed. When people we love are going through unpleasant or difficult issues it is also hard not to feel an emotional attachment and question or judge why such things happen to them. By being open to a bigger universal plan you can stop resisting how life unfolds, which in turn reduces suffering and eventually leads to tolerance and acceptance. With that, comes more peace and harmony which automatically leads to more understanding and more love. There is no better way to live than this. Our higher selves always know what's best for us and we would do well to pay attention to that inner guidance and allow life to teach us our earthly lessons, so that we can grow stronger and raise ourselves to new heights.

I see simplicity in nature; one harmonious event after another. Some quiet and invisible, and others catching my ear's attention with their sounds. At those exact moments, just before my mind has a chance to label and describe what it is, I feel the true essence of what life is. I take comfort in the peace and harmony of the way it is. Those precious moments prior to sensory perception are timeless and beautiful, and therefore free of suffering and judgment of any kind. In the moment, you are truly free to allow life to unfold as intended.

Nature does not need electronics or sports cars, or 24 hour movies on demand so why should we? How many of you would exchange your material things for natural pleasures; work a bit slower and fewer hours in exchange for less stress and more time to spend doing what brings you the most joy? Would you rather spend more time with loved ones or be out in nature instead of buying the latest iPhone and keeping up with the latest fashions and trends? It doesn't take a lot of money to be content and happy. When I was a kid all the adults would visit and socialize together quite often, and it didn't require much money to have a good time. There was no need for a pub or restaurant. One family would simply invite a few others over and sometimes each couple would bring over a salad or dessert they made at home. The only thing they really needed was each other's company. Those were good times. How many of us have the time these days to just get together with a few friends, whip up a few homemade snacks and just talk? Or exchange ideas, brainstorm a solution to a problem or just keep company with someone who needs it?

It's about what you need rather than what you <u>think</u> you want. Buying a new gadget or piece of jewellery may seem exciting at the time, but that won't keep you feeling truly content and satisfied for very long. Materials are temporary. I have quit my regular job and moved to a new city, and I have no idea what my new source of income will be like, but I know it was the right thing for me to do. After almost nine years of commuting to work (taking about three hours of my time a day) I finally realized that I don't need to spend my life in an unconscious and unhappy state for the sake of a mortgage. I know that I will be taken care of in divine order, and all I can do to aid in that regard is to look for and recognize other opportunities that will lead me to my goal even if it's not exactly what I have in mind. I have to move forward and learn from whatever comes my way.

Take only what you need instead of worrying about having enough. The universe has more than enough for everyone. Remember, we are all on different paths and should not be comparing our lives to those around us. We all chose our lessons to learn from as well as teach one another, and we need to keep ourselves from being distracted by unimportant things as much as possible. All it takes is that first step, done consistently until it feels natural.

Once you let go of fear and do what is appropriate for the whole, you open up a pathway for the universe to bring you what is most appropriate for your growth. We cannot always control our lives; we can only allow life to live through us and teach us what's needed for our evolution. Keep things as simple as possible. Do whatever you can for your loved ones but set your boundaries. Find that perfect balance between work and play and stick to it as best you can. When you find you can't, just take a step back to evaluate how to get back on track, and when you're on track you'll help others to get there too.

Children are experts at being in the moment and keeping things simple. They give their full attention to what they are doing in that moment. What a wonderful way to live. They can teach us so many things that we have forgotten. Simple things, but very important things such as true priorities. Kids really just need each other and a good environment to be content, a meal when their bellies tell them it's needed, and some loving attention when they hurt themselves. They don't concern themselves with yesterday or tomorrow and rightfully so, because they are not there. All their focus and energy is on the simple thought of right now. They seldom hold grudges or worry about whether they will have time to get something done tomorrow or the next day.

One of the reasons we make our lives more challenging than they need to be is because we tend to focus on fitting in with other people's ideas and goals. We are not meant to achieve and learn the same things or have the same material circumstances. Find out what your path is and focus on following it regardless of what those around you are doing. It is better to follow a path of wisdom than a path of intellect. It is not about how much factual information one can accumulate and recite at will, or how many projects one can manage at the same time. Rather, it is about how conscious we can be at all times and how united and cooperative with life we allow ourselves to be. Gaining awareness of our true, higher selves is what counts and is what will bring us the most harmony and happiness.

Isn't it ironic that the concept "simplicity" is something we all know the meaning of, yet it is something that so many of us struggle to maintain in our lives. There is great value in making things simple because complexity can cause one to lose focus and veer off track. Too much detail can lead to confusion and too much analysis is paralysis. Too many opinions cause conflict. Complication causes uncertainty and insecurity and many of us don't like to decide among too many choices. Simplicity allows one to feel in control. Plainness is obvious reality itself and it gives a sense of understanding.

One who is able to translate complexity into simplicity has power. When you present things in a more understandable form you diminish uncertainty and help make things clearer. However, when you do this you are still personally responsible. We tend to trust those who help us understand and reduce our doubts, and we often ask them what choices we have and what we should do, but we should never delegate our decision making to anyone. It is you, your interpretation, and your decision that determines what is best for you.

The sand on a beach and the stars in the sky are simple, yet boiling an egg is complicated if you have never been taught how. The most complex thing for us seems to be change - the unknown is complicated. Taking things as they come is simple, foreseeing what will happen can be complicated.

When we have less we want more, and when we have a lot more a part of us seems to want less. So which is it? What are the more important things in your life? Keep it simple and do what is appropriate for the moment! I invite you to take a few minutes for yourself and make a list of a few things that you feel are no longer necessary in your life. Anything at all, whether it be a chore, a duty you've given yourself because no one else was willing, or perhaps a spending habit that's gotten a little out of hand. Or maybe even a job. Anything that you feel is causing you unhappiness. Evaluate the things you are juggling in your life and do some decluttering and reshuffling. A change can be almost as good as a holiday. Take personal responsibility only for what is yours, and when assisting others be sure not to stretch yourself to thin otherwise you may end up not helping anyone, including yourself.

Effective communication is vital as well. If something is not clear to you, ask for further clarification because it is too easy to make quick assumptions. Also speak your own truth so that others will understand where you're coming from. If you want to be listened to, you must then listen in your turn. Many of us were told from a young age that we should listen before we talk - this is why we have two ears and only one mouth. Can this cycle of communication be any simpler?

9.

Honour & Integrity

For me, honouring yourself and others means to live from your higher (divine) self and to be of service to humanity. Honour involves respect for yourself and others and living as truthfully as you can, and also accepting your strengths and weaknesses as well as all the lessons and mistakes you have ever experienced. To truly honour is to accept all imperfections for there is balance in everything.

When we make a commitment to do something and we don't do it, a part of us loses faith in ourselves and our integrity, without us even realizing it. When we are not being true to ourselves our life force gets depleted and when this happens we don't have enough energy or stamina to follow through on the things we need to be doing every day. It is vital to think, speak, and act out of love at all times so that your energy remains high enough to propel you into taking right action on what needs to be done, in order to reflect who you really are. We play too many roles for society to the detriment of all. We are human and naturally have attachments to certain people and things but we must learn to release our hold on them so that we can live a more genuine existence which, ironically, will bring us closer together. This tribal mentality we experience is one of the things we need to overcome and we must work diligently and consistently at realizing our own truths and living in accordance with them, so that we can share our authentic selves with the world. By tribal mentality I mean a group or 'herd' mentality - where people tend to live and act in ways that fit in with, or please, other groups of people in order to feel accepted as a normal part of society. This is not honouring yourself or anyone else.

It does no good to anyone by holding yourself back or playing it too safe. We are here to grow and experience for everyone's benefit and this involves uncertainties and taking risks (aka following your intuition). It also involves allowing others to learn from their own choices without interference, even though we may mean well. The more we let go and trust the more we are free to honour our lives and get closer to spirit. Simply keep your focus on how *you* honour and express yourself and let others do the same, as they see fit. Let the light in you acknowledge the light in others.

When we act out of love there is no right or wrong, merely lessons learned. When we leave our personal opinions and judgments out of the way we open ourselves up to choices that are best for everyone concerned. Others may disagree with our actions or show resentment towards us but it is important to allow them to express their feelings and respect where they are at. It's not easy being the catalyst in someone else's life lesson but know that by stepping up and taking action you are doing their soul and yours more good than anything else. Not being and expressing who you truly are is a disservice to everyone. If someone doesn't recognize that you are acting out of love for them don't despair or judge them. Allow them to honour themselves when and how they feel appropriate. They will discover their own integrity in their own way.

Our problems don't come from outside sources - they start within by our own choice. When we create a problem we create a barrier that prevents us from seeing the bigger picture and the only one who can resolve a problem is the one who has the problem. I'm not saying that you cannot ask for help or advice but I am saying that you are responsible for your life and your outlook. You choose how to feel or act at any given moment. Acknowledge and honour your feelings as they arise so that you can express or be your authentic self.

A number of years ago I had to be the catalyst in a lesson for a couple very near and dear to me but it took two years for me to finally speak up and act on it. I allowed an arrangement between all of us that was not good for my personal boundaries, out of a sense of compassion and obligation. I believed that I was doing what was best for all concerned and I knew that they would have done the same for me if I had been in their situation.

As time went on, I felt the resentment slowly build up inside me. When it got really bad I would work on calming myself down and focusing on positive things to settle my mood, and I would also count my blessings. This would usually work and within a day or so I felt my normal self again. Since I was the only one who didn't like the way things were, I believed that I was the one with the problem and therefore I needed to work on my attitude. I would experience resentful moods from time to time which I believed was just my ego resisting the way it was. But gradually the resentment got worse and I realized what my real problem was. I was not honouring myself by speaking my truth about how I felt. How could I expect things to change by not being honest with myself and those around me? I felt that if I had spoken up others would feel bad and be put in a difficult situation that would not be for the good of all concerned. That was my assumption and judgment, which did make sense from a material perspective but I did not consider the bigger picture.

Eventually I could no longer contain myself, and when I finally did speak my truth to those concerned I started to feel better, although they didn't. I wasn't sure how my relationship with them would be going forward or whether the situation would change at all. But, I knew I had to be open and honest about how I felt, and also to accept the outcome no matter what. They too were now experiencing a lesson but soon accepted their situation and the next step they needed to take. I was merely the messenger or source of that lesson.

A month or so later, I spoke with them again to confirm that preparations had been made for our arrangement to come to an end within the time frame I had given, but their reply was that it was not happening and to my shock and surprise, I lost my temper! That very rarely happens with me. I was infuriated while trying to enforce the decision I had made for them. Although my intent was in the right place I was not so impeccable with my attitude. My boundary had been crossed and I showed zero tolerance. In my anger I even said that if this was the way it was going to be then I would be done with them for good once our arrangement did come to an end. I felt quite disappointed with myself for not using the knowledge and awareness I have to control my reaction and emotions, but soon after I expressed my regret and apologized. I explained that it was not them but rather the situation that I was unhappy about, and I told them that I loved them. But the hurt and the shock was now felt and, to put it extremely mildly, I was in the dog box. They took it very personally which I accepted and respected. And then, to my relief they honoured my terms and our arrangement ended a week later. It took me two years to have the courage to speak my truth about this - two years! I now know that I took right action and that, not to be judgmental, there had been a number of opportunities for them to take personal responsibility. But they chose not to and they had gotten comfortable.

If I had not followed up with my decision and stood firm about my boundaries nothing would have happened and my truth would have been lost in the wind. Lessons usually come to us in the form of other people and we need to focus on what the disturbance is trying to tell us rather than who the disturbance is coming from. I had finally honoured my feelings and it felt appropriate and good because I did it with love. I still don't know when the best moment to speak my truth would have been or whether I should have denied as much assistance in the first place, but I do know that divine order takes care of everything. What's meant to be will be. Period. For now, I will simply love them from a distance until our truths meet up to interact once again; but next time I had better be very conscious about it and respond with more love and compassion.

If you're not sure, let go and let God but be sure to honour all by speaking your truth whenever you feel the need. Your feelings are communicating with you all the time and you need to pay attention to what those feelings are trying to show you. To me, honour means expressing my own spiritual understandings, so it has nothing to do with right or wrong. As I've mentioned, everyone is a piece of the whole truth experienced in many different ways, so live yours straight from the heart without fear or judgment and you will give the world exactly what you were meant to - your authentic self.

Integrity is another vital part of who we really are and it is meant to be demonstrated in all that we do, so that the collective consciousness (or human race) can move forward and thereby create a better world on this beautiful planet of ours. A person's integrity says a lot about their true intentions and their commitments toward others. Just consider the word itself for a moment: it's similar to the word "integrate", which means bringing things together and combining them into a whole. So basically, your level of integrity will determine how positively or negatively you contribute to everyone and everything around you, and this will in turn create the world that you experience.

Integrity is one of the things that helps us to improve society and strive for unity. For me, it is like a powerful guide; it helps to keep me on the right path and encourages me to think and act more selflessly and more cooperatively toward others. It sits within my soul, patiently waiting for an opportunity to offer me guidance or to remind me of a higher purpose for being, especially when I have to make a selfless or uncomfortable choice. We live in such a busy, rushed society and often work in such demanding and stressful jobs that it can sometimes seem difficult to act in this way, even with simple things. I have noticed how one little oversight or lack of caring from one person can snowball into feelings of judgment, negativity, and isolation for a whole group of people and I am guilty of this myself. And even though I have noticed some lack of integrity on someone else's part I do realize that I have the power to either fuel it or counterbalance it by showing more integrity in all that *I* do. Leading by example is the way to go I think.

When you do things with integrity you align yourself with spirit and you allow your higher self to express its desire for you and for the betterment of those whose lives you touch. Acting in this way helps to overcome ego and selfishness, and encourages more love and consideration for others. It is a positive form of pride in that it brings a sense of accomplishment and contribution for the betterment of all, and it has nothing to do with status or comparison. This is something that should be applied to the most mundane, simple, and humble tasks as well as the most complex, influential, and risky responsibilities. Such behaviour can only encourage cooperation and respect among us. Whenever you make a commitment or an agreement with someone make sure that it is in alignment with your beliefs and morals, and that will make it easier to honour and accomplish.

Of all the characteristics most desired in a leader, integrity is generally identified more frequently than any other trait. That makes sense, doesn't it? If people are going to follow someone, whether into battle or in business or ministry, they want assurance that their leader can be trusted. They want to know that he or she will keep promises and follow through with commitments.

I'd like to share an example of a man from the biblical times who exemplified integrity. His name was Samuel and he was regarded as a man who exuded integrity. After having led Israel for decades, Samuel addressed his people by promising to repay anything he had unjustly taken from anyone. Even more impressive was the people's response. Not one person rose up to make a claim against him. Samuel's personal integrity permeated every area of his life and it directed how he regarded his possessions, his business dealings and his treatment of those who were weaker than himself. Samuel held himself accountable to the people he led and he opened himself up to the scrutiny of everyone with whom he ever had dealings with. As a result of this practice, Samuel's leadership has become legendary as this story has been told and retold throughout the centuries.

But integrity doesn't just apply to leaders; it applies to everyone. In today's society however, it seems that promises and commitments have become optional and we often seem more concerned with convenience. People give lip-service to the importance of character, but they have the idea that when things get tough, the rules can be changed and commitments may be discarded at will.

People such as Mother Theresa, Ghandi, Jesus and the Dalai Lama have told and demonstrated how important it is to honour our commitments. It always comes down to the issue of character, not just words. Integrity is not just doing the right thing; it's a matter of having the right heart and allowing the person you are on the inside to match the person you are on the outside. We need to become disciplined in our actions because disciplined people can do the right thing at the right time, in the right way for the right reason. So many of us have been burned by relationships, or by people going back on their word, claiming that they said something when they did not say it. This can make you cynical if you're not careful. Sometimes people let us down because there is a discrepancy between what they claim to believe and how they actually live, but the divine power within you will never let you down because the integrity of Source never changes and is not governed by external circumstances or conditions.

Integrity points to a consistency between our words and our ways, our attitudes and our actions, our values and our practice. What a person does will have a greater impact on others than what he or she says. People may forget 90 percent of what someone says, but they will never forget how that person lives. In this life we may not attain perfection yet, but there should be progress toward the Source that we came from. In other words, give careful attention to your behaviour and your beliefs. Make sure they match. Constantly examine yourself to see whether or not your walk matches your talk. One of the best ways to discern whether or not we are making progress is to ask ourselves, "How do I live when no one's looking?" It's easy to look like a person of integrity when people are watching, but do I live my private life with the same level of consistency as I live my public life? It's possible to live one life publicly and another life privately but that's not integrity. In the end, we become what our desires make us - who we become reveals what we really desire. If you desire the praise of men, then you will become a certain kind of person. But if you desire only what God desires for you, then integrity will need to become a priority. Every one of you has this in your heart because your higher self comes from God; you just have to choose it and live it until it becomes second nature.

10.

Free Will

In a sense, free will has a masculine and a feminine energy
to it. A controlling of the environment and the freedom or
allowing of emotional expression; thoughts and ideas that
need to be respected and implemented, and feelings that
want to be honoured. Our personal free will is part of our
challenge in redirecting our focus from the material world to
the spiritual world. It is there for us to utilize in the highest,
most selfless way for the benefit of others. We must reach the
point of <u>willing</u> to be more authentic and selfless; we cannot
be forced by unconscious discipline. Without free will there is
no real choice. Naturally in our teens and young adulthood the
ego's influence is very strong and our choices tend to be self-
focused, but as we mature and discover more of our gifts and
abilities we are then faced with how we choose to use them.
On a daily basis we are given the choice of serving our earthly
desires or serving humanity. Your occupation, for example,
can certainly be a major part of how you contribute to the
betterment of others but what you do is not that important;
the reason you do what you do is! When you are about to make
a choice, accept a job, or decide what course of action to take,
always focus on *why* you are making that particular choice.

Are you merely trying to satisfy your own needs or is there a passion or something meaningful that you want to share? Make it a habit to regularly check in on your motives in order to uncover what your true desires are.

Free will is a most wonderful gift to have in life but it does come with personal responsibility. How selfishly or selflessly we use it will determine our spiritual progress and sense of true happiness, and not just in our present lifetime. Our spirit is eternal, everlasting. The effort to move closer to God is required every day and can only be made by you. You alone choose how you live and deal with your life. You have free will to do what you like but you have no one else but yourself to thank or blame for your level of happiness. If you want love and happiness, then that is what you must send out into the world. You can only expect to receive what you give out. You may have known of someone who has been able to act selfishly, even for an entire lifetime, but that won't last forever; what goes up must come down. Free will holds a great deal of power and influence. Every choice we make affects the whole, no matter how mundane or insignificant some of those choices may seem. You will never know the full extent of the impact that your choices and actions will have in the world. The challenge of exercising your free will in the most positive caring way will always be there. It is part of being human and it is there for your spiritual evolution. Our 'soul' aim is to surrender our ego's will (desires) and allow ourselves to express the Divine will through us. This is how we bring ourselves back to our original authentic state (as the image and likeness of our loving creator).

And now for something quite the opposite. There is also a very different perspective on free will which is fairly uncommon in Western cultures and that is, there is no free will. It is an illusion. Well, at first glance this is something I don't completely agree with, but when I look beyond the words and give it some deeper consideration, I begin to see another perspective. Perhaps all of my choices I have, and ever will make, have always existed in the world of thoughts, and the ones I believe I have yet to make are merely waiting to become manifest in the physical world. It's as if my entire physical existence, from birth to death, together with all my choices and actions has already been mapped out, and my human awareness is still catching up with my 'future' choices as they unfold in the physical plane, through yet another illusion called 'time'. Linear, or clock, time is how we perceive and add the unfolding of events to our awareness (or memory), and since our awareness is always expanding it makes sense, in a way, that we don't yet know all of the choices we are destined to make. And since everything exists or takes place in the vertical (present moment) I must admit that there seems to be validity to the idea that we don't really have free will.

So, if you are still on the fence about which of these two perspectives is true, like I am, here's my idea of reconciling the two: since I cannot predict the future events and challenges that I am yet to experience, or the choices and decisions that I will be making, to me it still 'feels' like I have the free will to avoid them or make them when they arise (or most of them anyway). Not knowing all there is, now, leads me to believe that I can still influence my own path as well as the lives of others, thereby giving me a sense of having some control. I think most people feel that free will is basically having a certain degree of control over their lives. It doesn't really matter whether only one perspective is true, or whether both are one and the same truth. What matters, to me, is that I can be happy either way. Consider this: if life itself were viewed as a dance then most of us would likely see ourselves as the dancer, but the truth could be that every one of us is the dance and life is simply dancing through us all. Does it really matter though?

11.

Awareness Of You

Awareness is what helps you move forward in life and when you are fully aware, in that moment you are able to glimpse at a much bigger picture of life, even if just for a few seconds. Your attention is focused only on this very instant and not on anything else, past or future. Becoming aware only requires a split second and the more you practice it, the better at it you become. The length of time that you are able to remain in this state will increase with practice and if you choose to make this a habit you'll find yourself becoming more proactive instead of reactive, meaning that you will respond to events and people the best way you can in the moment with more clarity and focus, rather than reacting in the same or similar way you have in the past. Even if the same event or person crosses your path for the third time, you can choose to respond even better than you did on the first two occasions. This is especially helpful when encountering negative or stressful situations. Being aware helps you to appreciate life a great deal more because you notice so many more things you'd normally dismiss or overlook. Awareness is the way to better, more manageable experiences which can only be brought to fruition by you. Practice makes the master.

You are constantly creating or avoiding happiness for yourself and others so it is vital that you always be mindful of how you are projecting your energy. How you use it is so important in your everyday life because it shapes your future, your health, your happiness and your ability to grow and evolve, and it also impacts those around you. If you choose to put out positive energy in all that you do and say then you will accomplish a lot, have better experiences and feel more content with life. Your efforts in the present affect your future experiences.

Be aware of your feelings at all times because they indicate the type of thoughts you are having and may also indicate whether you need to change your view about something. This is your body's way of trying to make you aware of whether your thoughts are serving you or not. If there is anything you feel that you are lacking from life, send it out to all those you come into contact with and know that it must make its way back to you. Consciously put positive energy into everything you do, even the most boring or insignificant tasks. If there is something that you are doing in which you absolutely cannot find any positivity, then it's time to stop and focus your energy on something else. You may have to remain where you are for a little while longer or you may have to roll the dice and move quickly, then see where it leads. Regardless of the situation, what matters most is the type of energy you give out so it makes sense that you should avoid the things that do not enable you to bring out your best. Your energy has a lot to do with the way you experience life as well as the way others experience you, and although it's not possible to control everything in your path it is possible to control how you accept and deal with it. We are constantly affected by the energies of our surroundings, such as the people we interact with, the places we choose to go to, and the things we focus our attention on.

The company we keep probably has one of the most

influential effects on our energy so try to be with like-minded people whenever possible. However, if there is someone in your presence whom you feel does not put out a positive vibe, don't let it bring yours down but don't let yourself judge too quickly either. Simply keep sending them your own loving energy. What they do with it is up to them but what you do with yours is your responsibility. Everyone has their own vibe or mood and we should be respectful of that. If a person is showing anger toward you for example, you have the choice of whether to accept that energy and retaliate, or let it go right through you and respond with loving energy. If you are being attacked you have every right to defend yourself, but what's important is the way you do it. If your defence involves hatred towards your attacker, then you are taking on negative energy and missing the opportunity for your soul to learn from the experience and possibly help another to resolve an issue that is troubling them. However, you can certainly take action that may seem harsh to that person and yet be necessary, as long as you are doing it with the best of intentions for them. An attacker could be trying to (unconsciously) show you how they have been mistreated and may be looking to you for healing, but if you are not aware enough you could easily miss an opportunity to help someone heal.

You are creating <u>all the time</u> so try to always be aware of what (thoughts & deeds) you put out there. Remember, like attracts like, so if you continue to send out positivity all the time you will attract more of that to yourself, and those around you who tend to be more negative will either raise their vibration (become more positive) as a result or move out of your space. Also be mindful of the places you go to. Make a point of going to places where you feel positive or at peace, and if you have to go somewhere that tends to have negative or draining energies make sure to ground and white light yourself before you enter (basically, be aware of your physical surroundings and protect your own energy field, or thoughts, from other people's vibes). Sometimes I still get hit by a bad vibe when forgetting to do this, but as soon as I find my mood or thoughts being pulled in a negative direction I acknowledge to myself that these are not my beliefs nor a reflection of who I am. Then I replace them with loving positive thoughts and project that around me.

The things we focus our attention on are so vital because they are the things that we become. If you find yourself regularly focusing on something you don't like, go deep within yourself and ask what you can do to change your thoughts about it. Make it a habit of focusing on the things you do like in order to keep your vibration up. Some days this will be more challenging but the more you try the better your mood will be. We are constantly exchanging energy with our environment, both consciously and subconsciously, and for that reason I cannot emphasize enough how important it is to be aware of the way you think or project your energy. Like most things it does take effort and practice but it does pay off. You may be wondering how you could possibly control your thoughts while you're asleep? What often happens is that the thoughts (which are things) you are thinking about just before you go to sleep will continue floating around in your subconscious, so it's a good idea to make sure you focus on positive ones before retiring to bed as they will have an impact on programming your new reality when you awaken. Never go to bed angry. Day or night, your thoughts are continually fed by your energy so make sure to practice being aware of what thoughts you would like to become manifest in your life.

12.

Allowing

To be in a state of allowing is one of the natural laws of life and it involves allowing all things, all situations, and all people to be as they are even when other people do not allow you to be who you are. It involves surrendering to life instead of trying to control it. To many people, surrender generally implies giving up or failure when, in fact, it is just the opposite. It is a powerful action to take and it has a valuable purpose. It means letting life experience through you rather than trying to choose or control the experiences you want. To surrender simply means to allow things to be as they are for the moment. You may have an opportunity to take action in order to resolve or improve a situation, or you may not. Either way, remaining in a state of allowing will help you to better deal with whatever life gives you in any given moment. You don't have to like it or be able to rationalize it, but by not resisting or denying what is happening in your life you can understand what it means to allow life *'to be as it is'*. The spiritual reason for this experience is to help us recognize and accept higher opportunities and learning that we would otherwise overlook or choose to ignore.

We may not appreciate all the lessons that our souls have chosen for us but we do need to take them on at every opportunity, because if we don't they will keep coming back, and each time they will be less comfortable than before. I know, because avoiding is something I've been very good at in the past. When I resist or fight something, I may think that I've won but deep down I realize that the only way I can really win is to allow 'what is' and learn the lesson. Once we are able to listen to the spiritual voice within and trust the wisdom of our higher, selfless guidance, we begin a journey of empowerment and realize what or who we are truly capable of being. Surrender your resistant thoughts and feelings to make space for what you really need.

We have spent so many lifetimes placing values and judgments on things which are material and temporary that we so often miss the subtle signs leading us towards greater enlightenment and better choices for the whole. Give yourself time to consider your judgments and attitudes towards others. I believe that by accepting people for who they are helps us to understand that we are all here to make our own unique contributions toward a better life for all and that without each other, there cannot be a better life.

Fear also plays a part in our challenges which are there to test us and give us opportunities to grow and improve things, but fear can be overcome. We all have the ability and responsibility to make choices and to accept the consequences thereof, and part of our moral duty is to help others *whenever* we are divinely guided to and not when we happen to feel like it. What people really need now is inner peace but so many are far too concerned with their ego selves to allow enough of this wonderful gift to flow through them and onto others. It is such a vital energy that helps keep us in a state of spiritual, emotional and physical well-being. It is there for the taking and it doesn't require as much effort to attain as you may think; it begins within just by consciously choosing, and can then be spread out around us by something as simple and contagious as a smile. We can show peace instead of anger or argument to those who disagree with us and we can choose inner peace when going through experiences that we find very challenging or sad. As I've said, what you feel within you is what is projected out into the world and onto others. Peace is a high vibration that works in harmony with all life and it encourages cooperation and goodwill. Those of us who choose to live in this state automatically open up to the flow of love and contentment into our lives. If faced with giving up something of physical value or convenience in order to achieve peace then it is worth it, for the physical world is ever changing and we would all do well by not clinging onto it.

The benefits to being at peace with oneself include better mental and emotional well-being, more confidence and receptivity, and a greater acceptance of our life's experiences and the people in it. It also brings more clarity and patience which are both valuable tools in learning to connect with our spiritual side in order to strengthen our connection with the Divine. We have all experienced tumultuous times and it may be unreasonable to expect feeling perfectly at ease all the time, but one can still choose to make peace with whatever is, for the moment, until that situation changes.

Showing peace takes so much less energy than showing anger yet it is sometimes so difficult to do when faced with negativity or unconsciousness from others. But if we just recognize these situations as opportunities for growth we can make a conscious effort to respond more calmly and sincerely whenever faced with such challenges, and by doing so we will surely bring more inner peace to ourselves and those we interact with. This will not always be easy but it is most certainly possible with determination and practice. And on those few occasions where we fail a little bit there's always the next time to start fresh. When one is at peace the greatest opportunities and choices become available to you. Without it the mind is disrupted and your thoughts are scattered making it very difficult to make the highest and the best choices for the good of all.

Resistance brings disharmony but cooperation will sooner or later reveal the state that we so often desire. The task of being at peace with yourself keeps on presenting itself for your growth; if there were peace all the time we would cease to appreciate it as much and become complacent. Another thing to remember is that it's not the end result that's most important, for there is never really an end, but it is how you play the game so to speak. Your ongoing efforts to improve and strengthen yourself through this life are key to reaching new heights. Allowing inner peace to reside within you can occur in an instant - just by bringing yourself to a state of acceptance in that moment. Forget the past and leave it there where it belongs. Don't wonder about the future because it will never come. That leaves us with just the present moment, always nice and short. Now that your awareness is narrowed down to the split second of right now, allow a nice breath of inner peace to flow into you and just hang around. Keep doing this whenever needed and you will learn that inner peace is but a breath away. When you are completely aware and in the moment you are open to experience any positive state of being you choose, for suffering can only survive with time.

When we allow ourselves to be at peace we are open to letting countless blessings come into our lives. If we are not feeling at peace we put up barriers for ourselves blocking positive changes from occurring. The peace of God comes to those who continuously and tirelessly seek it. If it takes 50 attempts in a day to achieve it, do so, for some days are more trying than others. But you _will_ find peace if you really choose to. Remember, the best way to do this is to first be at peace with what is. Show others that this is possible no matter what your circumstances so that they too may find inner peace in their lives, and in turn share it with their loved ones as well as others they don't even know yet. This will also help us become more focused and better recognize our soul's deepest desires. The more we follow our heart's calling and evolve as life intended us to, the easier it will be to learn about what we've chosen to accomplish in this life, and why. This will lead to other positive attributes being developed and strengthened within us, and can often result in a better state of physical health too. Our physical well-being is linked to our state of emotions and often reflects the level of inner acceptance within us. Our peace or non-peace will find ways of showing itself to us through our attitudes and our bodies, and we need to pay attention to this and determine the best course of action to take when we do not feel that we're in a state of allowing. Whatever we feel on the inside will surely manifest on the outside so it is important to be aware of, and manage, how we are feeling at all times.

Whenever we experience suffering, whether accidental or seemingly intentional from other people, just see it as one of life's tests on your consciousness. Tell yourself that this too shall pass, and don't focus too much on the outcome. It's the little steps we take, one by one, in dealing with the apparent suffering that's really important. Our reaction and our ability to accept the external situation will determine how much peace we can allow ourselves to feel within. If you suffer from a serious illness, know that even that cannot stop you from feeling the love and companionship of a friend. If your new car gets rear-ended but all you suffer is a fright and some bruises, be glad that you're still around to hug your loved ones and eat more chocolate. If you lose your job, know that life is making space for new challenges and activities and new people to come into your life. The more we understand that both positive and negative experiences are necessary in order to grow, the easier it is to recognize fear for what it really is and the better we're able to push through our personal barriers and stay on track with our destiny. Nothing others do is because of you and when you are immune to the opinions and actions of others, you won't suffer. Simply do your best in any situation and don't judge yourself too harshly.

Achieving something always takes effort, which makes it all the more worthwhile when you get it, and when you need to achieve the same or similar thing the next time you may not have to make as much effort as you did before. So, if you regularly put in the effort it will often become easier for you to achieve inner peace when encountering further challenges. When we find what we are looking for, or when we achieve the state of allowing that we've been wanting, we should rejoice and express our gratitude but not cling to it and feel disappointed when it leaves us. All things are temporary and need to be appreciated as such. There will be many more opportunities for us to have positive and peaceful experiences. We just need to look more closely in order to recognize them, even in places or situations that seem uncomfortable or negative. Try to see an opportunity in any discomfort. If you can be at peace with your inner state of being, you will become far less phased when faced with difficult situations, and find more instances when you are able to counteract resistance. This also allows an opportunity to reflect and better understand why certain things are the way they are. Life is revealed to us in stages and we cannot predict or expect to know how the future will unfold. It is up to us how we deal with it and how we allow life's experiences to live through us. So, will you surrender and allow yourself to discover who you really are?

It's important to listen to your feelings and to trust what your heart tells you because that will encourage you to act, and therefore own those experiences as well as learn from them. Allowing life to flow and express through you won't guarantee an easy or painless journey but it will strengthen your soul, and bring you closer to God. I usually like surprises or new challenges but I sometimes catch myself judging whether I'll accept them or not based on how they make me feel. This can be tricky sometimes as ego tries to disguise my natural instincts with doubt or fear. Be wary of comfort zones. When things are going well, look or ask for opportunities to spread that wellness to others, and when things are not going so well think about what you need to learn or change in order to bring you from that to peace again.

The key is to allow the connection (or oneness) of all life to teach you and evolve you, and not to forcefully push your separated ideals onto others. Sometimes you are the teacher to another but take care that you deliver your message or lesson to them from a place of love and not from your egos intellect. Every one of us is both a teacher and a student and we must allow ourselves to move freely between these roles, and the more we allow and accept from life the closer we get to the source of higher understanding. Allowing is not necessarily a passive or defeated state. It takes great focus and right action. First, you need to focus on what you have an issue with; what is disturbing your natural state of well-being? Second, is not to lay blame on yourself or anyone else, and realize that the problem is actually an opportunity from your soul to learn and grow. Third, understand that taking any action may not always be possible or appropriate right away. Simply accept the moment as it is and allow life to bring you the solution at the right time. Right action could mean surrendering, removing yourself from an environment temporarily or permanently, or confronting an issue by speaking your truth to those concerned. Whatever the case, be sure to ask your higher self what is most appropriate in that moment.

To be in a state of allowing does not mean simply spending your time being, observing, and waiting for life to work out everything for you. You must actively contribute and take right action to enable you to align yourself with whatever you are trying to allow. No amount of physical action will compensate for resistant thoughts when trying to manifest something. The universe is always manifesting your true inner desires so if you are not getting or experiencing what you desire, you need to examine your thoughts that are contributing to the manifestation of your current reality. It is also possible that you are in denial of your true desires. Learning to just 'be' does help you release resistance and connect with your spiritual self, however, you cannot live life without taking some form of action in the physical world. You are all creators of your experiences and you are telling life where you want to go and what you want to do. The universe simply manifests the reality that matches your predominant thoughts or beliefs.

Worry also blocks you from your desires because it is resistance. It is opposite to anything you wish to manifest because it is a negative vibration. One who resists perceives the situation as a real problem, something they can do nothing about, and they become stuck in the situation and think they have no way out. They allow this thought to take over and begin believing that they really don't have any means to resolve the issue. As they begin to feel this way about their situation they begin to think this is their reality. When that happens, they feel defeated and their feelings lead them to believe that they will remain stuck in their present situation. This is how self-limiting beliefs become embedded in your thoughts.

If your thoughts remain positive the universe can only manifest what matches those thoughts. Inspired action is derived from positive emotions and therefore can only lead to positive results. It is also very important to remain open to your desires manifesting in a variety of different ways so that you don't limit yourself from expecting something to come into your life via one particular way only, because you then block other avenues and opportunities. Allowing your life simply to be as it is means letting it openly express through your intuitive instincts, and listening and responding from your heart instead of your intellect or fears. It involves acting selflessly and inclusively to all and understanding that everyone is working on their own lessons in their own time, and to stand ready to assist them, if or when they choose to accept it. Only you know when you are ready to move forward from a particular lesson or situation; you cannot be forced to do so by anyone else.

Be careful not to take on the energies of another who is struggling through a lesson, for it is not yours and is not up to you to resolve. Do offer assistance or advice if asked but remain detached from that issue and allow the individual to choose their own course of action when they feel ready. We may seem to be able to control certain outcomes on the physical level but if we have not learned to act selflessly and allow the higher good for the whole to prevail, we will simply be given more challenging opportunities until we do.

I'd like to share an example with you of how this topic has taught me a very interesting lesson in allowing things to reveal themselves from a higher perspective and in their own time, i.e. divine order. I've had a couple of goals or desires for a few years now and I've found myself believing that I have yet to attain them. I felt that I've been getting closer to achieving them but didn't stop to consider that maybe I'm already living those goals to a certain degree and I just haven't realized it yet. You see, I have a particular view or mental picture of the way these goals should manifest for me. However, I'm already experiencing them at a certain level just not on the three-dimensional level that most of us live in and relate to. What I mean by that is that I don't have those goals exactly the way I want from a physical or material perspective, but I do have them close enough for me to experience happiness and contentment in my life, and to stay focused on moving forward and not being too comfortable and stagnant. If I did have it exactly the way I wanted it would be too exclusive (for my personal benefit only); I wouldn't feel the need to make enough effort to evolve to a higher state of being with the whole and I would no longer have those goals to aspire to. As

I've said before, the journey is the goal and the journey never ends. It just gets better.

Now I can see more clearly that if I adjust these same goals to be more inclusive and selfless the more likely I will experience them on an even better level. By letting myself see things in a greater light I am better able to recognize what I have already achieved. Even if spirit had told me all of this from the beginning, would I have gotten it then? Would I have said "okay, I'll do exactly that?" I don't think so. Simply knowing or being told a bit of insightful information is not the same as going through the experience of learning it. That's what allowing can do for you. So I'll just continue to allow as best I can and let life reveal an ever higher, more enjoyable level of my goals to me throughout my journey here and hereafter.

Many of us tend to have more materialistic goals, caused by a false sense of separateness from others and a need for security from a physical perspective. But if you really take a deeper look at your hearts desires, you most likely want peace, joy, health and love more than anything else. Without these things even a billionaire couldn't be truly happy. Our higher selves know what's best for us even if we don't always recognize it, so just allow your life to take it's natural course as best you can and allow the perceived problems to reveal their solutions at the right moment.

Being out in nature is one of the best ways to let ourselves reconnect with life and our divinity. Being at one with the natural world is what we were made for. Trusting and following our heart and gut instincts, listening to our bodies and acting on what they tell us. Out in nature people seem to awaken and absorb what is naturally a part of them, and allow themselves to negate time and instead go with the flow of the environment. They also talk more meaningfully and attentively as well as actively listening to one another. Whenever we cooperate as one, nature is occurring. We don't necessarily have to be in nature in order to do these things although it does help a great deal. We may not be able to be outdoors as often as we'd like to but we can always bring some of it back with us into our homes and our relationships. Nature is also energy which can be shared and spread wherever you go; interacting and exchanging energy with other people, animals and even plants. Walking barefoot in your backyard or at the park, or doing some gardening will instantly connect you to mother earth and enable you to feel at one with her. It's like a health tonic from life. Even breathing in some fresh air from outside will have a similar effect because it contains life force. Air is constantly moving and at one with everything yet it doesn't have form. It does have energy though - lots of it. Think about how much light, sound and scent it carries throughout the planet for all living things to experience, not to mention the oxygen for us and carbon dioxide for plants. It has to be one of the most important forces in nature.

Isn't it interesting that the things which are the most beneficial to us are the easiest to find and never in short supply. Most of them are also free yet why don't we consistently indulge in them? Why do we find ourselves going after the things that seem so elusive, so hard to have to work for, and so expensive? Why do we choose the hard way over the easy way? The answer lies in mistaking what we want for what we need. And even when we are choosing what we really need, we still have to determine how much of it we need. Too much of anything is not ideal for any of us. This also includes people. Once we have learned or experienced enough from certain individuals, life will guide us to other people who may need our help, or who will be able to teach us something. This naturally means being more selfless and sharing a little less of our time with those who are our closest ties and giving more of ourselves to new people coming into our lives. This is how we grow; by sharing ourselves with more people because we are all connected. Whether this is appreciated by others or not, we must still move forward as life intended for us. Time waits for no man.

If we allow life to live through us and go along with where it takes us, we are living naturally. It can be challenging but that's simply part of the road to success. By resisting or trying to control life is unnatural and only blocks us from our real glory, in other words, our true nature. It is important to understand and follow nature's laws for they apply just as much to people as they do to anything else. Many of these laws relate directly to the way we think, what we say, and how we do things. When we do any of these in a negative manner, it is natural for life to bring us things of a similar vibration. Animals and plants have no other option but to behave and grow as the type of animal or plant that they are. They merely follow the pattern or instincts of their species as nature intended. But we, as people, have the gift of choice and with that the responsibility to use it wisely for the good of all. We are not exempt from cooperating with nature for we are part of it.

Think of nature as a signpost for you to imitate. So many different species of life living amongst each other in a peaceful and natural way, just doing what they are meant to do. We can do this with each other too by following the inner guidance that comes from within. We just need to practice getting in touch with our intuitive state and following its lead until it becomes second nature. The key is by cooperating with one another and not competing or comparing. Always direct your focus inward and concentrate on your own responsibilities and on what feels appropriate to you, and follow through on those things regularly so that they become habit. It is up to others to do the same for themselves.

13.

Humble Kindness

One of the traits associated with being humble and kind is generosity which is defined as: *the habit of giving without expecting anything in return. It is the readiness or liberality in giving. Generosity can involve offering ones time, assets or talents to aid someone in need. It is not solely based on one's economic status, but includes the individual's pure intentions of looking out for the common good of society and giving from the heart.*

Generosity should reflect an individual's passion to help others. It is the freedom from meanness or smallness of mind or character. In Buddhism, it is the antidote to the self-chosen poison called greed. It doesn't take much to be generous toward someone else and it is one of the most natural things for us sentient beings to do. You could say it's programmed into our DNA. We were born to do this throughout our daily lives and expand the degree to which we show generosity as much as we possibly can. From offering to help carry a few parcels for someone, to a money loan, to giving a person a ride home, it doesn't matter how great or small the act. Merely the genuine desire to help improve the life of another, even if just for a few minutes, is wonderful enough. In contrast to greed, this act arises out of genuine love for others.

Understanding what is most important for society as a whole helps us to understand why we are in this world. We are not here solely to accumulate as many material possessions as we can or live luxurious lifestyles and be served on by others, however I'm not saying that being financially rich is wrong. What I'm getting at is that although there are many pleasurable activities and experiences to be had, and many conveniences that money can buy, there are also important tasks to be done for the benefit of humanity. By living more spiritually and showing humility we learn how to get in touch with our soul and discover what our creator wishes for us to accomplish and learn. There may be billions of individual humans on this planet, but on a higher spiritual level we are really all one. We are all divine sparks of the whole creation so it is in our best interest to see each other as extensions of our self and to treat others as well as we treat ourselves, if not better.

If any of us have an abundance of something, shouldn't we share some of that with someone who does not? This goes for anything that could be shared: materials, food, information, training, kindness, love, some clothing, or simply our company. We are all extensions of the same thing and therefore are all equally important. This is easy for us to understand but not so easy to practice on a regular basis. What a challenge it can be to share with someone who is not our kind of company. But that is when we need to be keenly aware so that we can learn to express our most selfless and deepest love for another, regardless of their attitude towards us or our opinions of them.

Being generous, just like loving or protecting, is what sentient beings do. At least that's one of the things they're supposed to do. It may seem trivial, something one does when they have the time or the inclination, but this simple inexpensive act can snowball into so much more. Togetherness, supportiveness, happiness, new friendships, the exchange of information, and even soul lessons are some great examples of the effects of being generous. It also gives people a sense of hope, a feeling of being appreciated, and maybe even a sense of moral obligation to do the same for others. Confidence can also arise from the giver or receiver of generosity. This expression of kindness is also one of the many ways to raise your vibration and that of another. When those you are generous to choose to pay it forward you may realize the effect that this can have on a global scale. Be humble in your giving to others; assist them without expectation or acknowledgement. Far too often people forget to 'humble up'. It's not all about you, it's about the whole - everything and everyone. All of us are here to enrich the earth and leave it in a better state than we found it.

Don't think that your individual efforts won't make a big difference because they always do. That's how it always starts - with you. Its old news that we're all connected so whatever you do, you do it for the whole world. Energy never stops moving, it just changes for the better or worse, so it makes sense that the more generosity that goes around the greater the quality of life will be on this planet. This act is selfless yet it also benefits yourself because the more of it you give, the more you will get back. It's as if giving is the same as receiving.

For me, one of the greatest acts of kindness comes from those who help heal the souls of others and share their insights about living more spiritually. It reminds me of when and where I first heard of spiritualism and what my life was like when that person gave me direction into the spiritual world. How little I knew about my soul at that point! I have learned so much since then, and met so many others that have joined the spiritual movement in search of their own path. How many others do *you* share your spiritual understandings with? Think of how many light workers and spiritual teachers have resulted from this very important and generous act of sharing empowering spiritual knowledge and healing. Just imagine how effective and widespread this knowledge has become and how it has helped improve the lives of so many. Anything can be spread throughout this entire planet simply by sharing it generously and unconditionally.

Do you ever find yourself thinking whether you are being too generous to someone, or debating whether a particular person deserves your kindness or not? When you feel the urge to express your generosity don't concern yourself with deciding whether someone has already received a lot of good fortune in their life and perhaps doesn't need any more, or whether it's appropriate for them to receive anything joyful or helpful based on your feelings about their personality or their actions. Being generous must be done unconditionally and should never be used as a bargaining tool because it will then be all in vain. Do things selflessly out of love for others without fear for your own needs. Don't try to bargain with spirit. Remember, the deed doesn't have to be huge, just do what you can. Just act from the heart without thinking or analyzing. Do as if you were God, giving unconditionally to whoever is in need at the time.

What more can be said about generosity? It is something that is innately within our souls and therefore needs to be expressed and experienced in this world in order for us to grow closer and closer to Source. It's just that fear has caused us to hesitate showing it, sometimes even towards ourselves. Some people hesitate to be kind to themselves out of fear of being selfish or greedy or that their loved ones will lose out in some way. Perhaps some tend to be too generous to the point of enabling others and thereby neglecting themselves. Being generous to yourself in the same way you are to others isn't taking away from anyone. It's quite the opposite, just like the way love works. Everybody is equal and the more genuine kindness you show yourself the more of it you will have to give to others. The Source of infinite creation is kind enough to have us all experience an eternal existence with as many opportunities and as much time as we need to become more kind and more loving to all. Can you think of anything as generous as that?

14.

Expectations & Obligations

From the time we were little children we were taught, trained and encouraged to do things a certain way and behave in ways that suite or please others. We were made to study and educate ourselves about subjects that were meant to help us have a better future for ourselves, and to learn about things that we will be expected to earn or will need to own in order to be secure and successful one day. Conformity and physical survival was strongly ingrained in us. Many of us often didn't question any of these things and simply assumed that those who were trying to show us the way knew better, and had our best interests in mind. And those who did tend to question things often faced resistance and disapproval. Society in general has been taught to simply obey and trust authority. We have unknowingly been giving away our power for too long, but now more and more people have become aware (more conscious) and realize that this has to change. It is time to start listening to your own inner voice and then acting on it. March to the beat of your own drum and blaze your own trail. Learn to trust your own intuition and take responsibility for doing so. In other words, live in your own power! Just do what you do best and leave the outcome of your efforts to the Divine.

Appreciate the way your life chooses to unfold - you are not always in control.

You don't need to place any expectations on yourself or others; we are all learning and evolving at our own pace, in our own time. We all make mistakes and people's attitudes toward you can change a great deal when you don't meet their expectations, but that has nothing to do with you. As long as you act from a place of love and do your best you shouldn't be judged. You need to live your own way and your self-worth cannot be determined by anyone else. When you agree to do things for people, especially the ones you are close to, make sure those actions align with your values. Never compromise your morals, for that can restrict you in so many ways and you can lose sight of your better judgment and limit yourself from important learning opportunities. Showing tough love to someone you are very close to is a perfect example.

Having deep-rooted beliefs and expectations that were ingrained in you early in life may have been appropriate or helpful at the time, but now you must re-evaluate how you feel about them. Doing things out of a sense of obligation to someone else is usually not a good enough reason and it can sometimes prove disastrous for your own well-being. It has to feel right for you now, because you are not the same person you were a few years ago; or even a few months ago. Circumstances change all the time and so can you, and for that reason I feel that the word 'obligation' or 'expectation' should be replaced with the phrase "what is appropriate this time?" Morally speaking, being obligated to tell the truth or treat people with respect is appropriate, but feeling obligated to keep company with someone who mistreats you in any way, even if that person happens to be closely related to you, is not appropriate. Yes, this gets sticky when family members are involved but you must honour yourself; always do what *you* feel is appropriate and forget about what others may expect from you. Remember not to put expectations on anyone else or make them feel obligated either. If you do, sooner or later you will be disappointed, for they have to decide what is right for them and act according to their own feelings and best understanding.

15.

Forgiveness

Forgiveness is about renewal and fresh starts. By forgiving we choose to let go of our own blockages, limitations, and negativity, and we release things from the past that no longer serve us. It is a conscious decision to renew our efforts to move forward by releasing the hurts and resentments that are keeping us from bringing out the highest and best in ourselves. Forgiveness is not conditional on getting someone to change their ways or to understand our perspectives and pain; it is a selfless act that we do for the betterment of everyone whether others recognize it or not. If we all had the same values and attitudes there probably wouldn't be the need for forgiveness. It's about letting go of the suffering and judgments lingering within ourselves and choosing to create a new and more positive outlook on life, as well as making changes to our attitudes toward others and their perceived imperfections. We often forget that we can be just as imperfect as some of the people we judge, only in different ways. Yes, some transgress more heavily than others, but who are we to try to measure and compare their mistakes - we have not walked in their shoes and faced their battles.

We can't change how other people act but we can change

how we deal with them. In a way forgiveness is also a very selfish thing to do, but in a positive sense because we are doing it for ourselves so that we can move on and live happier lives. We are not attempting to change the people that are, or have been, in our lives; it's not about others or the way we perceive their faults and their behaviours. They are merely our teachers who are reflecting something within ourselves that requires healing or improving. Sometimes we are the teacher for another but it is very important *how* we offer our assistance or advice to them, without trying to change them or getting them to act before they are ready. It is easy to point a finger at something or someone else when faced with a situation that we cannot accept but that is simply ego reacting to something that doesn't conform to the way it thinks it should be. We all have our own ideas of an ideal world and when we experience something or someone that goes against that, a part of us resists it or refuses to deal with it. This is natural for ego to do because it is programmed for survival mode. It places its own needs before anything else because it doesn't know any better. This is where we should pay close attention in order to respond from our higher self and not our ego. Recognizing the lesson is what's important and so is the way we handle it. The person or situation is merely the way in which it is being presented. Even though the transgressions and hurts we suffer usually come from people who are close to us or are known to us, we still have the responsibility to either learn the lesson or resent the teacher. Depending on the situation, one may not initially be able to choose the former but with patience and good intention just forgiving what has happened to you will allow the healing process to begin. Know that resentment is such a toxic and debilitating vibration which harms you far more than anyone else - it is not worth hanging onto!

If you can remain present enough to deal with a difficult person or situation as it arises and allow things to be as they are for the moment, you will be able to let that energy pass through you and release it. You don't have to agree with what is happening or have a solution right away but if you can just remain in a conscious, focused state by accepting the way it is, you won't find yourself resisting or blocking that energy inside you, but instead letting it take its course. By doing this you allow the solution to present itself at the appropriate time. The act of forgiveness then becomes almost unnecessary because you choose to live in the present without hanging onto any negativity from the past. Remember, what you resist persists. Unresolved hurts and resentments will keep reappearing until they are dealt with and released. Life lessons often come to us in the form of other people but it is usually not them we should be focusing on. They are merely messengers, like signposts directing us to look inward and examine the blockages requiring our attention.

By living and dealing with life in the present we can continually renew ourselves and let each day be a fresh start, free of old resentments and regrets and anything else keeping our souls from growing closer to God. Just make your best effort to be as loving, patient and understanding as you can every day so that it becomes habit, and when you find yourself falling short of doing that don't be hard on yourself or too judgmental toward another. Simply remind yourself of how you'd really like to be and let your higher self guide you through your day. When you are able to go with the flow of life's ups and downs you learn not to accumulate more unhealthy baggage that can distract you and hold you back, and this in turn allows you to be more aware so that you can better recognize older issues buried deep within that still need forgiving and releasing. Sometimes we can hold onto something for years and push it so deep within us that we forget how to deal with it properly, or even forget that it's still there.

Forgiveness is an essential part of human and spiritual life as it cleanses body, mind and soul, but if one remains in a state of unforgiveness for too long that blockage can and often does manifest itself in all three of these areas because it goes against our divine nature. Since our souls are all connected as one source of unconditional love it is in our best interest to regularly practice forgiveness for ourselves and others so that we can continue to make our way back to that perfect state which we came from. Yes, it is sometimes very difficult to forgive so if you find yourself trying to get past something that seems too overwhelming to deal with, just break it down into smaller steps to work on day by day and ask the Divine to help you. For a start ask yourself why you feel so bothered or angry about something that's in the past and remind yourself that what has already happened is beyond your control. Also make a point of not worrying about the possibility of similar things happening to you in the future. Thoughts are things so be mindful of what you draw into your consciousness. Keep your focus on just dealing with the present moment. Also create some affirmations for yourself to help program a new attitude and more positive beliefs for yourself. Perhaps the next step could be taking some time each day to ask yourself what could be learned from that experience. Quieting the mind and going within is a great way to gain insights and answers from your soul. Try writing down whatever solutions or insights come to you and do your best to put them into practice so that it becomes habit. This may take a bit more time than you'd like but it is a worthwhile exercise in order to work through problems and keep moving forward. Another thing you could do is to write down every old, negative belief you have about yourself or others and replace them with new and positive beliefs. Then shred or burn the list of old ones if it makes you feel better. Doing these kinds of things helps you to raise your vibration and reinforce your efforts to work through those issues that get in your way. Finally, be kind to yourself; you are entitled to take as long as you need to work through hurts and other struggles - no self-judgments! Real healing does take time.

When I need to work on forgiveness, whether it be for myself or others, I always get into a meditative state first and then bring to mind those people I need to heal with. As I picture them in my mind, I say these words to them: *"I forgive you and I release you; I hold no unforgiveness back. I am free and you are free, for we are one for eternity. I love you."* After that, I may also send them healing and well wishes (with my intention). You can also try forgiving others by speaking directly to those involved if you feel it is safe or appropriate, but forgiveness does not always have to be done in person. It is your intention that counts. This exercise may take just a few days or weeks or it may take a much longer time, depending on the severity of the issue at hand, but it does work. It could also happen that you reach a point when you feel you have totally released and forgiven someone or something, only to have it creep its way back into your life and become a regular disturbance again. If that happens, it is likely that you still have a few more layers to work through, so just get back to doing your exercise of forgiving again and keep doing it until you feel that you have let it go. And don't be hard on yourself either. Sometimes breaks are needed between layers of releasing, especially if it is something very deep rooted or painful. It's very important to allow yourself as much time as you need to work through forgiveness.

Forgiveness is like a seed. How much of it you sow will certainly result in how much your soul will reap, and whenever you heal you provide an opportunity for those around you to heal. Forgive whatever has happened to you and be an example of hope and strength to others. Show the world that everyone has free will to choose happiness, gratitude and peace because these things are natural gifts that come from within us, not from external or material sources. Every moment of each day is a fresh start so make the most of it and watch your life change for the better. The more spiritual you become the more inner strength you develop, and this allows you to handle life's challenges with greater ease and compassion. Think of yourself as being like a seed but with a particle of divine consciousness or infinite intelligence inside of you. From an outward glance we may appear quite small and seem unsure of how to make real progress in life, but within us we all have the power to grow in leaps and bounds if we are willing to allow ourselves.

We are here to evolve and life's obstacles and challenges are there for this reason. Our progress is determined by our effort and willingness to work together as a unit in the most loving way we can. We don't have to understand how everything works. We just need to accept our past actions and experiences for what they were and release them so that we can allow new experiences to take their place. With new experiences come new opportunities to respond in better ways, instead of reacting like we have in the past. Make a conscious effort to think, speak, and act in the best way you can going forward, regardless of what others say or do to you, and watch your ability to forgive and remain in the present moment grow immensely.

I'd like to share the following two quotes that relate to forgiving and letting go:

"The weak can never forgive. Forgiveness is the attribute of the strong." (Mahatma Gandhi)

"You can't reach for anything new if your hands are still full of yesterday's junk." (Louise Smith)

With each new day consciously renew your thoughts and feelings about everything in the most positive way and you will draw more like-minded experiences toward you. Forgive and let go of things that don't help you anymore so that you can replace them with new things that will serve you on life's journey. It only takes a moment to make a fresh start.

I want to share with you a quick story of a video clip I

saw on YouTube once about a group of people who conducted an exercise in the city of New York that relates to regret and forgiveness. This group placed a very large chalk board with a bucket of chalk in a busy part of the city with a message written on it saying "write down your biggest regret." As people walked by and read this some of them stepped up and wrote down their own biggest regret in life. Once the board was full the group that was organizing and filming this exercise approached the board to review its messages. The vast majority of sentences began with the word "not" and the rest began with the word "never". The regrets included things like "never completing my college degree", "not being honest with myself or my friends", "not going for an opportunity because of fear or uncertainty of the outcome", and "never telling someone how much I really loved them". Some passersby had also stopped to read these regrets, and a couple of people who had written their regrets on the board openly said "thank you" for the opportunity. All the regrets were then erased from the board revealing a clean slate. The message behind this was that it's never too late to forgive the past and start afresh.

16.

Grace

The law of grace takes precedence over the law of karma. Grace is the point at which your soul has understood a particular lesson (through physical experience). It is the completion or total understanding of a karmic condition or situation, and it occurs when you have allowed your higher self, or soul purpose, to express itself in the physical world as divinely intended. When you put your ego aside and forget about serving your own needs first when dealing with a challenge or difficult situation, and instead ask life what it needs of you, you are led to the path of grace, but you must then 'choose' to follow it, again and again, working through one distraction or illusion after another.

Attaining grace is like rediscovering your true self; it is the liberty of God to lead you through something to its completion so that you gain a complete and comprehensive understanding of it. This process often involves many steps, many attempts, some wrong turns, or poor decisions, but owning these experiences and recognizing them as necessary stepping stones on this physical plane helps you find grace. We all came from grace, fell from it, and came to this beautiful planet to reclaim it. We've been roaming and searching all over for it through the generations and now more and more of us are realizing that it has been right under our noses all this time, buried deep within our hearts.

One of the very first messages I received from a psychic medium many years ago was: "open your heart and your mind." That was it - short and sweet. I understood logically what these words meant but this message seemed so bland and basic I never thought of it again until years later. Opening my mind (expanding my consciousness) was the easy part for me, but as for opening up my heart (showing unconditional love), I had no idea how challenging this would turn out to be. Sometimes it still is but I'm a lot better at it now.

The persistence and dedication to just show up each day and pursue the very best expression of yourself will lead you to grace. A healthy balance of heart and mind will better enable your soul to point the way for you through your choices, options, and personal responsibilities. Learn to trust the things you don't physically see that feel very real and alive in your core. Work through your desires and evaluate your wants on a regular basis to give you a better sense of what your true needs are. And since everything your soul really needs is within you, you job (or rather your purpose) is to uncover it and express it to the best of your ability each day. You will always have the option to show grace toward those who try to attack, judge, or inflict pain on you, but just know that a kind gesture, a compassionate ear, or even just a well-meaning attempt to give advice or some tough love could make the world of difference to someone's life - whether they recognize it or not. Never underestimate the power of planting a seed; I think all of us have needed that at some point in our lives in order to get where we are today.

17.

Manifesting

When you put something out there that you need help with, aside from being clear about what it is you want and keeping positive thoughts and intentions, you also need to take another very important step in order to help it manifest. And that is taking action. You need to do your part in the physical world to help accomplish what you need and also be open to it manifesting in ways other than the way you expect it to. It won't always just fall into your lap a few days after you've told the universe what you want. Thoughts have a certain vibration and words have a higher vibration, but actions have an even higher vibration than these. That is a natural law. Your words are your thoughts being expressed, and your actions are basically your words and/or ideas put into motion.

I learned that to get where I wanted, I had to take that first step by just starting to do 'something' and trust that the next steps would then be revealed to me at the appropriate time. In the past I was hardly moving forward at all because I was anticipating the complete solution with all the steps to come to me before I was willing to start taking action, and therefore was oblivious to recognizing the signs or means to get me closer to my goal. My expectation had narrowed my focus so much that I couldn't see the trees for the forest. So I decided to write a few things down that I could start doing now (some of which I had done before but quickly gave up on). But this time, as I began working on putting these few things into action consistently, I realized that I was now actively working towards a goal and the enthusiasm of it was raising my energy and motivating me to keep at it. Even though the direction was not totally clear there was now momentum in what I was doing, which meant that a new future for me was being created that would naturally manifest, sooner or later. I didn't know what the end result of my efforts would bring but my intention was in the right place. With this renewed energy and enthusiasm I was now better able to focus on manifesting the desired goal into my present reality, and my taking action was now allowing me to become more receptive to a new reality. Intention is <u>very</u> important when using your energy to work on anything. If you find that you've gotten a result that you feel is not what you desired, you need to take a closer look at your intention because your results will always match your true intentions.

There are three important things to do in order to create a new reality for yourself. First is the thought, or goal, and it must be as clear as possible. You need to know exactly what it is that you need to achieve. Then comes the word, which must be spoken clearly, truthfully and with the utmost faith. Whenever you speak of your goals to others proclaim them with complete certainty so that people will be aware of what you need in order to achieve them, and thereby be able to assist or provide you with better possibilities along the way. Thirdly, the deed must follow and be done consistently with the highest of intentions until the desired result is achieved; take whatever action you can each day that may bring you closer to your goal. This is the way to manifesting all that you already have within you. Another thing I will add is that your feelings need to be in alignment with whatever you are working on; you must be passionate about what you are trying to manifest for yourself. It is very important that you truly believe in it; accept that it already is, even though it hasn't happened or appeared in the physical yet. Most people, however, need to see something first in order to believe it, but that's not how it works. All the things you create, experience, and see around you first started off as a thought. The manifestation of anything is the final step, not the first one.

Manifesting doesn't only involve lifestyle and career changes. It can, even more importantly, apply to your outlook, attitudes, and overall sense of well-being. Who wouldn't want to view the gift of their existence in a positive light? Everyone has bad moments, some more than others, but would you rather be a bystander and just let life happen to you or would you rather actively participate in trying to create the best life you can for yourself? There are also many other things you can do to raise your vibration such as daily affirmations, regularly counting your blessings, meditating, singing, or just going for walks. Taking deep and focused breaths a few times a day also works well. I personally like slow breathing and absorbing as much sunlight as possible (even if I have to stay indoors). These little exercises don't take long to do and it's just a matter of making something a daily habit.

Another important thing to be aware of is the type of energies you accept from others when interacting with them. If you cannot agree with or be at peace with someone, don't let that affect you in a negative way. Everyone has their own truth and we should be respectful of that. If a person is showing anger toward you for example, you have the choice of whether to accept that anger and retaliate, or let it go. The same goes with disagreements; it's better to try manifesting kindness than trying to prove who's right. If you are being attacked you have every right to defend yourself, but what's important is the way you do it. If your defence involves hatred towards your attacker, then you are taking on negative energy and missing the opportunity for your soul to learn from the experience and possibly help another to resolve an issue that is troubling them. However, you can certainly take action that may seem harsh to that person and yet be necessary, as long as you are doing it with the best of intentions for them. Even when you help others you are manifesting a better world for yourself too.

We are all constantly exchanging and manifesting energy, both consciously while awake and subconsciously while asleep, and I cannot emphasize enough how important it is to be aware of what we are manifesting for ourselves. Like most things it does take effort and practice but it does pay off for everyone. You may be wondering: "how I could possibly control my energy (thoughts) while I'm asleep?" What often happens is that the thoughts (which are things) you are thinking about just before you go to sleep will continue floating around in your subconscious for a while, so it's a good idea to make sure you focus on positive ones before retiring as they will have an impact on programming your new reality when you awaken. Day or night, your thoughts are continually being fed by your energy so make sure to practice being aware of what thoughts you would like to become manifest in your life.

18.

Spiritual Giving

Spirit is like a sieve; it helps a great deal to act in this manner. It does not hold onto things and allow them to build up. Rather, it gently refines and softens all that comes its way while at the same time letting it pass through and change into something else. It never forces or blocks anything from moving forward in its own way and time. Spirit is most patient and stands ready to help guide and smooth out anything that comes to it for help. It does not react to or judge things. It simply allows them to flow right through it as it takes in the experiences.

Spirit is also like a grid of energy, offering a bubble of protection over all life and connecting it with everything else. In the grand scheme of things we all have the same origin and eventually we'll all return to it along with the knowledge and understanding of all our life experiences. Spirit - is life - is energy - is one with everything. Therefore, it is also something that all of us are responsible for handling. By this I mean how we use it, share it, and learn from it. I've certainly received my fair share of it over the years (in the form of assistance, money, guidance, support and much more) to my personal benefit and I realize the importance of giving back the same to others. Everything is energy and so it must be given and received by all. Spiritually speaking, when one of us benefits in any way all of us do but we need to keep sharing our gains and gifts with others in order to keep growing. Energy is a dynamic, constant and moving force and it needs to be circulated in order to do its work. When it becomes blocked or stuck it ceases to fulfill its purpose.

People cause all sorts of blockages for themselves without realizing it. I used to worry about having enough for myself in order to feel happy and financially secure which caused me to be too frugal and too afraid to give to others first. I had to ensure I had enough, and some extra, before I was willing to give. This also applied with my time. As a routine I did what I felt like doing first, when I felt like doing it. This selfishness also resulted in me being afraid to take risks and hesitating to try new ideas or different experiences, which led to a great deal of stagnation, not to mention stress, frustration and unhappiness. Over the years I had blocked so much energy from taking its natural course that I wasn't growing much spiritually at all. By making the choice to serve and give more to myself and less to others, I created an imbalance and blocked the path to receive even greater gifts and allow others to benefit more from me.

Maintaining a healthy balance in any area of your life is key to positive spiritual growth. Give much of yourself to helping others and be grateful for everything in your life, no matter how small or simple it is. Sometimes we don't realize how valuable something is until we no longer have it. Learn to enjoy things as they come to you as well as when they leave you. Life is full of give and take. Give thanks and take nothing for granted. Give without remembering, take without forgetting.

I'd like to share the following brief story about a group of board members of a spiritual congregation in the U.S. who were holding a meeting to discuss their financial needs for the coming year. One of the members suggested they each talk about the people and places they give money to and share why they chose them. It was an interesting exercise. One woman said that she sends a goat each year (paid for by her contribution to her charity) to a needy family overseas. Another mentioned that she writes a check to the American Cancer Society in memory of her father each year. Others give to their colleges, the United Way, the Red Cross, and other well-known charities. Some focus their donations on one cause to which they feel very dedicated, such as an animal rescue group or an environmental organization.

What we do with our money is a sign of who we are and what we love. Our individual money trails are reflections of our priorities, experiences, hopes, dreams, and wealth. As one Benedictine monk said, *"Abundance is not measured by what flows in, but by what flows over."* When most of us are being forced to make hard decisions about where to put our limited resources, what do we reveal about who we are by what we give? It's not how much we are able to give that matters as much as that we give regularly. Even if our current contributions can't match what we have given in the past, we can continue our commitments and our intention to remain connected to giving. Generosity is a spiritual practice that reflects an attitude of heart and mind. Here are just a few examples of potential ways to help others:

- put a small bill or coin in a place where you can reach it quickly. Give it away to the first needy person you meet, without stopping to evaluate how the money will be used. This simple practice cultivates the habit of giving without thinking about what you might get back. It reminds you that everything you have is a gift to be freely shared.
- build giving into your daily choices. Have a generosity jar in your home. When you resist the impulse to go out for an expensive dinner or buy a new jacket or dress,

put a couple of bank notes in this jar. Instead of buying a new toy for your kids put that money in the bank for them which could be more helpful for them in the future. Periodically empty your generosity jar and have a family council to decide how to distribute it. Be creative in how you fill the jar and how you give its contents away. You can have a lot of fun with this practice.

- get friends or co-workers to join you in giving. Whenever you get together for a social, have everyone put a couple of coins into a kitty for someone or someplace in need. Or start a friendly competition at work to pool together some money for a particular cause or charity and see whether your company is willing to match your contribution.

- inspire yourself by reading about ways of helping others which is a blessing for both the giver and the receiver because it creates a connection with the vast expanse of humanity. Giving money is not the only means; generosity can also involve caring for the environment, offering love to a homeless animal, sharing your possessions, forgiving and being patient with others, providing information or understanding, as well as many other selfless acts.

Some of you may know of the movie called "Pay It Forward" which shows what happens when an 11-year-old boy is given a school assignment, to think of an idea to change the world and put it into action. The boy decides to do a good deed for three people and then ask each of them to "pay it forward" by doing a similar deed for three others. Before long, his project becomes a movement, demonstrating how a little love and kindness can really make a difference in the world. The universe operates through dynamic exchange - giving and receiving are different aspects of the flow of energy in the world. And in our willingness to share that which we seek, we keep the abundance of the universe circulating in our lives. I'd like to share the following quote with you by Deepak Chopra: *"I will give something to everyone I come into contact with, and so I will begin the process of circulating joy, wealth and affluence in my life and in the lives of others. Today I will gratefully receive all the gifts life has to offer me."*

Sometimes when you go through difficulties, you learn much more from them than if things were easy. This is why people go through difficulties on their path, because it throws up all kinds of emotions and things within, which they didn't even know they had. Sometimes people are tested to the limit and in all this, if a person helps other people, then spiritual help comes back to them. It's a give and take thing. Everything that exists does so in cooperation with or as part of other things, and together they form the whole. So if you are thinking that you can receive spiritual knowledge and assistance without helping in any way, without helping other people or helping to spread it, then that is a mistake because you break that flow of give and take which exists in nature. It exists everywhere; nothing works on its own. If you simply want to receive spiritual knowledge and do nothing with it, you will receive it in isolation, and the supply will be cut off. When nutrients and nourishment are cut off from something in nature it dies out, and that is exactly what happens with spirituality. So it's worth looking at what you can do to help others to progress spiritually, and to be part of the whole. In that way you're going to get help too, and this is how to move forward and grow spiritually. By doing this, it's going to help the world. It's going to help people to change - people who are looking for information and direction on awakening, people who are going through great psychological struggles or other difficulties, and are looking for something that will enable them to change. And the means to give them that knowledge is here, the teachings as well as the lessons of other people that can be passed on to humanity. Anyone can become part of this change that is so important and so needed.

However, many people are not really interested in changing fundamentally. Many like the idea of being more aware, of being more spiritual, but real change takes a lot more than that - it means discovering things in you that you don't like to see, admitting your mistakes, and essentially humbling yourself. Even though many don't really want to change, it can be sufficient enough that those people who are willing can really do great spiritual work. It's about providing an opportunity for real spiritual change to those who are drawn to awakening and any of us can make a big difference in the lives of others. Just ask yourself what you can offer to support those in your community to better themselves. There are many diverse and well-meaning spiritual groups needing your help to spread a more inclusive, spiritual way of living. I encourage you to give a helping hand in whatever ways you feel appropriate in order to keep the spiritual energy moving. Keep circulating the gift of giving and the receiving can only make its way back to you.

19.

Deep Contemplation

This is about continuous self-discovery that never stops. For me, it's like an ongoing two-step process consisting of prayer and meditation. When I pray, I am sending out my seeking or my requests for assistance into the vast realm of the Divine. When I meditate, I am waiting patiently for the insights or answers to my searching. I throw my boomerang far out into the astral plane, expecting or hoping for it to return bigger and better than before. I know it will; but always in divine order. Once the boomerang leaves my hand my control over it ends and the bigger picture begins to weave its plan for my delivery. What will the outcome or the answer look like? Will I accept it or give my boomerang another throw, hoping for another, better option?

Contemplation reminds me of the Serenity Prayer by Reinhold Niebuhr: *"God grant me the serenity to accept the things I cannot change, the courage to change the things I can, and the wisdom to know the difference."* I wonder which of the three parts of this prayer is the hardest to live by? I guess that depends on where you're at in your personal growth; perhaps most of us experience all three as the toughest, but each one at different stages in our lives.

I had struggled for years with focusing for any decent length of time. I seemed to have some difficulty keeping my attention on my immediate surroundings and the people in it, but I had no trouble drifting off into the unseen world and spending hours with my thoughts and imagination. Learning to focus really well proved to be a big challenge for me, especially when I was first learning to meditate. Without this invaluable tool I wouldn't be able to contemplate on a deeper level, nor do the kind of energy work that I so love to do. Being able to explore the depths of your being is essential to your personal growth. When I was younger, a few of my school teachers thought that I was simply a naughty or disinterested kid who chose not to listen. I wasn't naughty, but I definitely was not interested in most of my school subjects. However, when I was doing one of my favourite things I had no trouble at all focusing; I could spend hours working on an interesting or creative project. Only much later on in life though did it seem to me that my ability to diligently focus on the task at hand depended a great deal on how engaged and stimulated I was by that activity. Makes sense right? How can anyone be expected to focus and contemplate on something deeply if it does not resonate with them? The school system of education which I experienced is a perfect example. The old school, disciplined approach to learning, combined with limited options of subjects to learn or choose from, left little room for individuality and intuitive guidance.

As for all the jobs I've had, there were times when the work seemed fine and I felt content to be there, but that wouldn't last long and I'd grow bored or dissatisfied, or both. To make things even more difficult, I still had no idea what I really was interested in. All I knew was that it was something I couldn't see or touch. That's not much to go on is it? So, I had to spend many years doing and experiencing jobs and other things that I didn't like in order to help me get closer to figuring out what I did want to do. No experience is ever a waste though - there's always something to learn from it and there are no coincidences. Sometimes we'll never figure out how or why we ended up in a particular place or situation, and certain things will remain a mystery no matter how much time you spend contemplating or trying to rationalize them. And even if you find that you have now found purpose and meaning in what you do, that could change at any point. Life is all about change, and change is constant. All you can do is deeply appreciate and live the life you have *'now'*.

When you are contemplating anything about life you need to be in a state of allowing, and cast aside all resistant thoughts. Have no preconceived ideas or expectations, at all. Any planning or scheming needs to be forgotten about. There must not be any personal investment in what may be uncovered from within you because that is where your true (spiritual) gifts lie, and these are the gifts you are meant to be giving to others. Remember, it's all about what blessings you were born to share!

My soul 'speaks' to me so softly, and it is often difficult to follow, let alone hear, its guidance. Contemplating on my souls wishes requires a lot of discipline and courage. If focusing my aim on the greater good of others isn't trying enough, there's also hoping my bag of courage is big enough to get me to act and do what is required of me. Sometimes contemplating the deepest parts of my soul is like trying to clearly see the bottom of a shallow stream that has just been crossed by a herd of buffalo. It can't happen in seconds; I must wait until all the mud has settled to the bottom again before the water becomes clear (my emotions must not be invested in any way). Yet other times, it seems pretty clear and straightforward. But that's only half the job. My will is what drives me to do, or not to do. Am I willing to accept whatever the divine offers, and allow it to unravel in my life without attempting to manipulate it in any way? Control and contemplation do not work well together. Pondering the deepest mysteries for truth or understanding requires letting go completely and refraining from placing any value or preference on them. It is an acceptance of whatever 'felt' senses come to you, as well as allowing these felt senses to change into something else without trying to understand it all logically. It is a deep exploration of your spiritual essence that cannot always be clearly defined or described, because it is far beyond words and far deeper than mental concepts. To me, having and accepting an emotional (or bodily felt) sense or understanding seems to be a much closer fit to what deep contemplation is all about; it's as if the mind is not just contained in the brain but is rather a medium for us to connect with the highest realms of consciousness in order to appreciate life's mysteries, as well as uncover all the illusions in order to see what's actually real.

20.

Destiny

We all have a life plan to complete on this earth and it is our responsibility to discover, bit by bit, who we really are (our authentic, divine self) and what we need to be learning and contributing to the world. All our life lessons and challenges are chosen by the soul and the more effort and attention we give to working through them the better we can start to understand what they mean to us. Every person has countless opportunities to achieve higher levels of wisdom and unconditional love no matter what stage they are at in life. Our true, original state is all-knowing, all-loving, selflessness and our destiny is to return to that state once we have completed all the experiences and lessons of our life's path. Our difficulties are gifts from the soul to help us get to that state of bliss; it has to be earned no matter how long it takes. Every one of us has a unique list of challenges to go through and as much time as we need to deal with them. Some of us have to hit rock bottom before we are willing to surrender and take a closer look within ourselves to discover what we need to be doing or working on, while others may start coming round to a sense of higher purpose in a smoother, more gradual way. However, no one's path is better than that of another. We all have certain things that are predestined for us and we will face them at some point no matter which direction we take in life. We can take the most direct and challenging approach to deal with things that bring us discomfort, or we can choose an easier, more roundabout way.

We are all destined for greatness and unconditional love, every one of us. In fact, we are already that, but this cannot be realized or measured in just one lifetime. We have all experienced very positive and very negative things for our soul growth and we need to understand that this is all a necessary part of our destiny in having human experiences. All of us will, sooner or later, come to understand unconditional love through our experiences, and reunite with the source of creation from which we came. We are all meant to achieve perfect consciousness, but no one will ever be forced to search for God's way. You can choose to remain exactly as you are for as long as you wish, thanks to the gift of free will, but the lessons or opportunities for growth will continue to present themselves in your life. Comfort zones can be nice or at least give you a sense of security, but they can also be addictive, and they do get in the way of your personal growth. As I mentioned before, life needs to continually change in order to be life. There is always more for you to learn and experience - that is your destiny.

21.

Q's & A's

1. **What is our deepest and most important purpose in life?**
   To discover who we really are at the highest level (our soul) by expressing and acting out our most honest feelings at all times and in the most loving and selfless way we can.

2. **Where is spirit from?**
   From within all of us and everything we can imagine. Every thing, being, thought, and action is spirit. Nothing in life is separate from it.

3. **How does spirit manifest?**
   In the physical, such as people, animals, plants, mountains, oceans and clouds; in thought, such as ideas, opinions and memories; in feelings, such as love, joy, sadness, hunger and pain; as well as many other forms of energy, such as dreams, sounds and psychic messages. Spirit is energy and everything in the universe is energy, therefore everything anyone could ever conceive of is spirit.

4. **Why does spirit manifest?**
   To experience all there is. Although spirit knows all there is to know, simply knowing everything is not the same as experiencing it all. Experiences are for enjoyment as well as learning.

5. **Why are there some experiences that are not enjoyable at all?**

   In order to fully understand and appreciate something, both polarities of it need to be experienced. For example, if there were no darkness we wouldn't really realize and appreciate the wonder of sunshine and daylight.

6. **Why does spirit only come to earth and not to other planets?**

   Spirit actually does exist on other planets but not necessarily in physical form. There are many undiscovered planets out there and many plains of existence both here on earth and elsewhere which cannot be physically seen, heard or touched. We share this planet with many realms of life forms.

7. **Why does spirit try to communicate with us?**

   Usually they want to help us and guide us with our earthly lessons as well as bring us proof that there is eternal life after our physical bodies expire.

8. **Are spirits from God or are some bad ones from somewhere else?**

   Yes, all spirits are from the Divine Source of all creation which is known by many other names, such as God, Allah, The Source, Yahweh, etc. There are some spirits that act in negative ways but they too have the choice to move into the light and become more positive energies, and eventually they will. Remember, with all things in life, both extremes (both positive and negative) need to be experienced. No one can ever fail and remain blocked from the highest good for ever. Some may struggle and battle for what seems their whole life, but all will get there eventually.

9. **What is spirit all about?**

   Spirit is, first and foremost, about pure, unconditional love and it wishes to gain the fullest experience of such love through each and every soul that has and ever will exist. Spirit is connected to everything and therefore continuously gains more understanding and emotional experience of this love.

10. **When will there be peace on earth?**

When most of us consciously choose to live peacefully and act in ways that benefit everyone and not just ourselves. We must do this even when others do not follow suit or agree with us. If we insist on waiting for others to act first then we will be waiting for peace for the rest of our lives. Remember that everyone is at a different level of evolution and you can only come to know peace by living it to the best of your ability.

11. **When I die what will I do next?**

You will never, ever die. Your physical body will eventually expire but you will keep evolving, learning and experiencing in ways that we can't yet imagine. Our purpose is to evolve and gain a greater understanding of all there is. When our physical bodies die we cross over to a non-physical world with a much higher level of understanding about ourselves and our true purpose. There, we are able to review our entire physical life and discover what we could have done better in order to fulfill our destiny. We live on forever and so have countless opportunities to grow closer to God.

12. **Why do good things happen to bad people and bad things happen to good people?**

Nobody is essentially bad - we are all from the one, same source of creation (a.k.a. God, Infinite Intelligence, life). "Good" and "bad" are simply judgments we all make about most things, but it is important to understand that we are not to judge at all. Rather, we must understand that everyone is at a different level of understanding with their own set of experiences and lessons to go through, in divine order.

13. **What is divine order?**

This basically means that all things happen when and how God intended and we should not judge or criticize as none of us really knows all the details of life's plan for us. We may feel that we are owed more enjoyment or have earned bigger rewards than the ones we've gotten, but there are bigger things our souls are working on that we have yet to learn.

14. **How can we feel happy about life if we don't have the same loving relationships and material comforts and securities that others have?**

There is a great deal more to us than the physical world and part of our mission is to figure out what our spirit needs to learn from all the people we interact with, even if we don't like some of it. We need to discover true happiness within ourselves and realize that all material/physical things are temporary and of lesser importance. This can be very difficult to appreciate from a human perspective. All we ever really need is already within us and is waiting to be discovered and shared with the world. When one discovers their higher purpose and follows it, he/she will feel truly happy with life.

15. **Where exactly is the highest source of love and light?**

It is deep within all of us and everyone is making their way to it at their own pace and in their own way.

16. **Can one choose to learn their lessons faster and easier?**

Yes we can, as long as we do our part. The more effort and dedication we put in the better, and we can also ask for our lessons to be combined and to be learned energetically (through observing others) rather than physically. We can request that our lessons be experienced in the mildest form possible (for example, a fender bender rather than a head on collision), however there are some things we're meant to experience that are pretty much set in stone.

17. **Why is the kind of music we listen to so significant in our lives?**

Sounds, like everything else, have vibrations (both positive and negative) and since we give such a large part of our attention to hearing it is very important to monitor which music we allow to enter both our consciousness and sub consciousness. Paying attention to the way a particular song makes you feel or think is a good way to determine whether it is appropriate for you.

18. **What is the most important thing in your life?**
Serving others. What you give out you will surely get back although it may not necessarily be in the same way. By helping others you are helping yourself because we are all from the same source.

19. **What is the nearest thing to God?**
Unconditional love.

20. **How does one know when they are acting in accordance with their soul's desire?**
When it feels appropriate and natural even if it doesn't make a lot of sense or fit in with society's ideals. It basically just feels right in that moment.

21. **When do you know you are with God?**
When you do not have to think with your mind or make a judgment of how it should be. When you simply follow your heart and allow life to just happen to you. When you act on your instincts instead of your logic, and when you serve and love others ahead of yourself.

22. **How do you get to know who you (higher self) truly are?**
By listening to, and acting on, your gut instinct before your mind has a chance to judge or influence it. By allowing life to take its course through you without any resisting. Resisting is the ego (easing God out) and so is wanting. Your true self desires nothing for itself because it has and is unconditional love. Go with the flow. We don't have to accept a negative incident or person, but we do need to accept our feelings about it. By responding with your most loving and selfless ideas you will discover you true divine self.

23. **How much love can you give to others?**

That depends on how much you have for yourself. The more you truly love and appreciate yourself the more love you will have to share with others.

24. **If you have lived a troubled or regretful life how can you achieve perfection (godliness)?**

By accepting who you are and taking personal responsibility for your life. If there is anything about you that you are not happy with, you have the choice to change it. Forgive yourself and release all that is no longer a reflection of who you are now. We can all choose to make better choices going forward and make our way closer to perfection, one step at a time. Mis-takes are a natural part of life's journey.

25. **Why do people have the free will to choose not to follow the path of God?**

God loves us unconditionally and therefore wants us to experience things and make choices as we see fit at any given moment. God desires for us to discover the gift of unconditional love in our own way and at our own pace. If we did not have free will there would be no opportunities to choose and therefore no point to experiencing life on earth. God is unconditional love and as such can only be reached by choice.

26. **How do you know when God is 'speaking' to you?**

God often speaks to you through your feelings so it is really important to pay attention to how you feel at all times so that you can focus on what you need to learn. Most of our lessons come to us in the form of other people but it is important to focus on how their words and actions make us feel rather than focusing on the people themselves. People are merely the messengers of our lessons as well as mirrors that reflect things in ourselves that we usually don't recognize, and we should not take anything that others say or do personally.

27. **What is it that people fear the most?**

    The unknown or future. Because people tend to think about all the things that they don't want in their lives instead of thinking about what they do want, they concern themselves with these thoughts manifesting in their lives. Many people also tend to fear what they do not understand (spiritualism is a good example). Anything that is outside of, or contradictory to, one's beliefs is usually rejected and considered threatening or negative.

28. **What is meant by a person's vibrations?**

    It is the energy which emanates from them. It is the essence of who they are and what their intentions are.

29. **Can a person change their vibration?**

    Absolutely. All it takes is conscious effort and action, done consistently. This can be done through practising meditation and making positive lifestyle changes. The more effort that is made the sooner your vibration will begin to change. It's all to do with one's intention. In addition, by changing your vibration you automatically affect those around you and also help them to start changing theirs.

30. **What else can a person do with their vibration?**

    They can use it to heal themselves by learning how to discover and work on their spiritual needs, as well as help to heal others by learning how to give spiritual healings.

About the Author

Andrew was born and raised in South Africa and immigrated to Ontario, Canada soon after getting married. He only became drawn to and involved in spiritual practices at the age of 35, but his intense curiosity and determination has led to the discovery of a life changing passion and a journey of self-reflection, research, spiritual education, public speaking, and teaching. This ongoing journey has allowed him to hone his spiritual coaching and psychic abilities; and motivational teaching & healing, together with mediumship, is what he loves to do most.

Printed in the United States
By Bookmasters